MINDFUL PARENTING FOR AUTISTIC CHILDREN

UNDERSTAND ASD, OVERCOME THE CHALLENGES,
AND SUCCESSFULLY PARENT CHILDREN WITH
AUTISM THROUGH PRACTICAL DBT SKILLS AND
MINDFULNESS ACTIVITIES

CATHERINE L. ABBOTT

D1707378

CONTENTS

YOUR FREE GIFTS

Thank you so much for your purchase. The fact that you are taking time out of your busy life to read my book means the world to me.

Knowing how precious your time is and as a way of saying thanks for your purchase, I'm offering **The Ultimate Family Morning Routine** AND **The Ultimate Family Night Routine** for <u>FREE </u>to my readers as bonus.

These bonuses are **100% free** with no strings attached. You don't need to provide any personal information except your email address.

To get instant access just go to:

https://mindfulparentingbooks.com/free-gift

Or simply <u>Scan This QR code</u>

<u>AS AN ADDED BONUS</u> :

Dive into your child's mind with your **FREE** Copy of my e-book "**Raising Happy Children**"

Get your Free Copy in one Click:

<u>Raising Happy Children</u>

INTRODUCTION

You're sitting in the doctor's office, nervously fidgeting with your fingers. It's been weeks since the process started, going from the doctor to various therapists: occupational, speech, and a child psychologist. *Today is the day we find out what's happening,* you think.

When the doctor came with the diagnosis, you weren't surprised. You suspected it. Your child's always been different from others. However, as much as the doctor only confirmed what you deep down already knew, hearing the words, "Your child has autism spectrum disorder," shocked you to your core.

Suddenly, you're filled with a rush of emotions and thoughts. *Why does my child have to have it? How will I help them? How will I know what to do? I can't do this. Why did this have to happen to us?*

You go home, and every time you look at your beautiful child, you want to cry all over again. *I have to pull myself together*, you think as you grab your phone to do an online search. *I have to find ideas on how to help my little one.* Unfortunately, this online search leaves you even more confused, as it seems like every website's idea of how to parent a child with autism seem vastly different from the others.

"I have to get help," you tell yourself as you tuck your child in bed. As you watch your child rocking themselves to sleep, you're more determined than ever to make changes to your parenting style. If this sounds anything like how you felt when your child was diagnosed, you've come to the right place.

I've been in your position. I know exactly what you're going through. Seventeen years ago, my son was diagnosed with autism spectrum disorder (ASD) and attention deficit hyperactivity disorder (ADHD). This diagnosis left me confused. To say that it left me in a state of complete panic is a massive understatement. I felt unsure of the way forward. I had no idea what I should do or how I could help my son. I felt completely powerless.

I was set on giving my child the right care that he deserves, so I wanted to learn everything I could about both conditions. I was motivated and dead set on finding solutions that would work for both of us and would help him have the life and future he deserves. Along the way, I've made many mistakes, but I've used these to shape my expertise and parenting style. Luckily, we were surrounded by a loving family that made the effort to understand what my son was going through. As a result of this, my son could cope with the stress of daily life and even make some good friends.

Since I've seen the positive impact of certain changes to my parenting style, I'm passionate about helping others in the same situation. Nothing brings me greater joy than helping other parents of children with ASD, ADHD, or other mental health issues such as depression and anxiety overcome their fears and worries and deal with the challenges head-on. I'm a firm believer in mindful, interactive parenting and the impact that the techniques learned in dialectical behavior therapy (DBT) can have.

I set out to help others by writing blogs, speaking at events in the community, and publishing my first book in 2020. All of the tips I give others are based on my personal experiences, extensive research, and the wonderful success stories that I've been part of.

I truly believe that for parents to be able to help their children, they need thorough knowledge and a solid support system. Now, I want to help you overcome the challenges that your child's ASD may bring and help you avoid making the same mistakes I've made.

Whether your child has only just been diagnosed with ASD or you've been trying to help him with his symptoms for a while, the tips that I'm discussing in this book will help you overcome many of the challenges you might face. If you implement the tips and strategies I discuss in this book, you'll know exactly what to do the next time you're in a distressing situation.

In *Mindful Parenting for Autistic Children*, I've divided the information into three parts to ensure it is easy to understand and reference:

- **A complete overview of ASD**, not just the stereotypical information that's so often shared, but also the causes and how ASD may affect your child throughout the different stages of their life.
- **Tips on how you can help your child thrive**, including introducing tips from dialectical behavior therapy, how you can teach your child social skills, and how to accept your child with compassion.

- **How to overcome the various parenting challenges you might face**, including dealing with the stress you might experience and how to be more mindful in your parenting style.

Parenting, in general, can be a difficult and stressful experience. This can be even more true if you have a child with neurodiversity. Luckily, it doesn't have to be that way. The first step in raising a thriving and happy child is to truly understand what ASD is, as well as the symptoms of the disorders that fall under this umbrella term.

If you are ready to improve your parenting styles and give your child the life they deserve, let's straight into it.

1

LET'S LOOK AT THE BASICS

Autism and ASD can sound like very scary terms, especially if they are used to diagnose why your child's behavior and development have been different from those of neurotypical children. However, once you truly understand what this condition entails and why your child might behave in certain ways, it can help reduce the stress you might experience. This can help you stay calm during difficult times and know how to help your child overcome the challenges they may face.

A lot of the fears you may have about this condition might be associated with the societal stereotypes many people choose to believe about autism. The best way to overcome this is by educating yourself, not only on the condition but also on the stereotypes surrounding it.

To help you do this, we will start by giving you an evidence-based introduction to ASD to explain everything you need to know about the condition, the different types of ASD, how it is diagnosed, its potential causes, the early signs of ASD, and the societal stereotypes. We will also have a quick look at how ASD can affect your child before going into greater detail on this in Chapter 2.

WHAT DOES AUTISM SPECTRUM DISORDER MEAN?

ASD refers to a condition that results in differences in the development of a person's brain and nervous system. It can severely affect a child's growth, their social awareness and abilities, and their communication with others. They often struggle to make and maintain eye contact with others and may say things that are generally considered to be rude or inappropriate.

People with ASD typically struggle to develop empathy and, as a result, struggle to understand emotions and how others react to them. Even deciphering facial expressions can be difficult for people with ASD. They are usually extremely upset when their routines are changed, often don't want to be touched, and prefer spending time by themselves. They may also repeat movements, become overly attached to certain objects, and generally have a very good memory.

All of these symptoms can be directly linked to the brain development of a child with ASD. Studies have shown that the brain of a child with ASD will go through a stage of overgrowth during their first two years of life, particularly in the cerebral, cerebellar, and limbic structures of the brain (Courchesne, 2004). This overgrowth is then often followed by drastically slower or sometimes arrested growth, which often takes place during a developmental stage where neurotypical children begin to excel in language, cognitive, and social development.

This stage of arrested growth can then result in a child losing skills that they've already learned. This will often be referred to as a "regression," especially when children who haven't been diagnosed yet are discussed.

Furthermore, the difference in brain development is why the differences between a child with ASD and a neurotypical child often only become visible between the ages of two and four. It is important to always remember that ASD doesn't affect a child's intellect, as some stereotypes want us to believe. In fact, people with ASD often excel in math, science, memory, and playing a musical instrument.

TYPES OF AUTISM SPECTRUM DISORDER

ASD is an umbrella term to describe many different disorders with similar developmental and behavioral symptoms. This is why many people who are "on the spectrum," as it's often referred to, will behave and develop differently. For example, some people with ASD can successfully interact with other people, while others may be completely nonverbal. Some people with ASD will behave in socially acceptable ways, while others will continuously rock their bodies or clap their hands. Some will cope with life with very little support, while others will need extensive help.

It is, therefore, important to understand the different types of ASD so that you can better prepare yourself for the support your child might need. Even though there are many different disorders that fall under ASD, we will discuss the four most common ones:

- **Asperger's syndrome**: This is usually regarded as a very mild form of autism. People with Asperger's are often extremely intelligent, and as a result, they can achieve great success in their lives. They may have an intense focus on topics that interest them and can talk endlessly on these topics, but their interest may be very narrow. Generally, they're able to cope with life relatively well and may learn to manage their symptoms to such an extent that they can thrive with only limited (if any) support. They may, however, struggle in social environments and say things that others will deem inappropriate.

- **Pervasive developmental disorder, not otherwise specified (PDD-NOS)**: People are usually diagnosed with PDD when their symptoms of autism are more severe as those of Asperger's but less intense than those of autism disorder.

- **Autism disorder**: This disorder is more severe than PDD, and those with autism disorder will likely require more support to be able to thrive. People with autism disorder typically struggle with social interactions and communicating with others.

- **Childhood disintegrative disorder (CDD)**: This is the most severe and rarest form of ASD. Children with CDD typically start to develop normally, and then lose many of their skills between the ages of two and four. These skills can be social, verbal, and cognitive. Most children with CDD will also develop a seizure disorder, such as epilepsy.

CAUSES OF AUTISM SPECTRUM DISORDER

The exact cause of ASD is still being researched, and it is believed that, due to the complexity of the disorder, many factors can play a role in its development in a child. Let's look at some of the factors that may increase your child's risk of having ASD:

- **Genetics**: There are various genes that are thought to be involved in ASD, as these genes can result in genetic mutations, affect brain development, or how the cells in the brain communicate with each other. If you have a family history of autism, your child will be at a higher risk of having this condition.
- **Environmental**: It is believed that environmental factors can increase the risk of a child having ASD. This can include viral infections, medications, metabolic conditions, such as diabetes or obesity, or complications during pregnancy. The use of alcohol or drugs during pregnancy can also increase this risk. Some also believe air pollutants could play a role in brain development and result in ASD.
- **Age of parents**: It is believed that parents who conceive the child when they're older (over 45 years) can result in more neurodiversity in a

child, including ASD. This refers to both the mother and the father.

- **Other disorders**: Children with other conditions, such as the intellectual disabilities Fragile X syndrome, Rett syndrome, Down syndrome, and tuberous sclerosis, are at a higher risk of having ASD as well.
- **Low birth weight**: Babies that have an extremely low birth weight—typically before 26 weeks of gestation—have a higher risk of having an ASD.

Even though many people choose to believe that childhood vaccinations can cause ASD, researchers have been unable to find a reliable link.

People with ASD are also more likely to have other conditions, such as

- ADHD
- epilepsy or seizure disorder
- eating disorders
- bad sleeping habits
- gastrointestinal issues
- mood disorders, such as anxiety and depression
- fearlessness

Always remember that just because your child has ASD, it doesn't mean they will develop any of these other conditions as well. By giving your child the support they need, you will be able to greatly reduce the chances of your child developing another disorder.

EARLY SIGNS OF AUTISM SPECTRUM DISORDER IN CHILDREN

As I've already mentioned, most children with ASD will start to show symptoms between the ages of two and four. This is where clear signs such as not talking, walking, or playing become visible.

However, some may even have clear symptoms between 12 and 18 months, or even earlier. Many times, these very early symptoms will be ignored until they become more severe or obvious during toddlerhood, or parents may not even realize that their child's behavior can be early signs of autism.

Some of these early signs can include

- difficulty making and maintaining eye contact.
- not reacting to their name by the age of nine months.

- not showing basic facial expression, such as happy, sad, angry, and surprised, by the age of nine months.
- problems with following a gaze.
- not using basic gestures, such as waving, by the age of 12 months (one year).
- doesn't point to something they're interested in by the age of 18 months.
- not noticing when others are sad or hurt by the age of 24 months (two years).
- inability to imitate or take part in pretend play by the age of 36 months (three years).
- can't sing or dance by the age of five years.

As a parent, you should always look out for signs of developmental differences in your child. If you ever pick up on anything that seems atypical, it's best to discuss this with your child's doctor. In many of these conditions, early intervention can improve the outcomes of treatment.

While the signs above are fairly clear signs of ASD, your child may show other signs or exhibit restricted or repetitive interests or behaviors that could signal your child might be on the spectrum. If your child shows these signs, it will be a good idea to keep a closer eye on them and consult their doctor immediately if you're worried. Some signs you should look out for include

- lines toys or objects in a specific or straight way.
- repeats the same phrases over and over.
- always plays with their toys in the exact same way.
- focuses only on a specific part of an object.
- becomes obsessive about their interests.
- gets extremely upset by minor changes to their routine.
- repeats specific movements, such as rocking their body, flapping their hands, or spinning themself in circles.
- has specific or severe reactions to tastes, smells, and textures.

Reading through these symptoms and signs can sound very scary and intimidating. Your child is looking to you for guidance, so you'll have to be able to pull yourself together and look past the symptoms at the child who needs you. We will discuss various ways in which you can do this later on in the book.

However, one way of doing this is to focus on the strengths that can come with ASD, for example:

- Being able to remember details for a long period of time.
- Being extremely auditory.

- Excelling in math, science, music, or art.

DIAGNOSIS: WHEN YOUR EXPECTATIONS ARE CONFIRMED

There are no blood tests your doctor can do to diagnose your child with ASD. As a result, a diagnosis won't be made after a single consultation with the doctor. It will likely take weeks of tests and evaluations before the doctor makes a diagnosis.

Your child's doctor might notice some developmental problems during their checkups, or your child's teacher or caregiver may pick up on behavioral challenges. You might even notice that your child isn't acting like their neurotypical peers. Once you've started to suspect something is wrong, it would take your child to your doctor or their pediatrician to start their evaluation.

An ASD diagnosis is usually made after completing two steps. Firstly, your doctor will do a developmental screening. During this time, the doctor will look at your child's basic skills, such as moving, behavior, speaking, learning, and listening. If the doctor finds any developmental delays during this screening, they will move the process to the next step.

The doctor would likely consult your child's teacher or caregiver for feedback on their interaction with other children. Your doctor will likely also refer your child to other specialists, such as occupational therapists, speech therapists, and child psychologists, for proper evaluations. Apart from play therapy and hearing and vision tests, your doctor will likely order some blood tests to look for genetic abnormalities and to rule out other disorders. Your child may also be referred to a pediatric neurologist to make sure there is no other neurological condition that might cause their symptoms.

Only after all these tests have been completed will a diagnosis be made. Your doctor will then discuss the different treatment options for your child. This can include different forms of medication to treat difficult symptoms and therapy, depending on the severity of your child's condition.

COMMON STEREOTYPES OF CHILDREN WITH AUTISM SPECTRUM DISORDER

The societal stereotypes that surround ASD can make it more difficult to cope with the diagnosis and treatment, not only for you but also for your child. This is why it's important to understand these stereotypes and how there's usually little to no scientific evidence to support them. Once you understand these stereotypes, you can quickly tell when someone does not understand the condition and bases their knowledge only on stereotypes.

Let's look at some of the most common stereotypes about ASD that are often wrongly accepted as the truth:

- **There's something wrong with people with autism**: ASD isn't a disease like influenza that can be cured. There's no cure for autism. A child with autism will grow up to be an adult with autism, although they may be able to deal with their symptoms better as adults. Instead of seeing autism as a disorder, choose to see it as your nationality. No matter what you do, if you were born in Canada, you'll always be a Canadian. Even if you move to a different country, it won't change your nationality. The same way that there's nothing wrong with being Canadian, there's nothing wrong with being autistic, even if the symptoms of ASD can make life a bit more challenging.
- **If someone is nonverbal, they also can't understand**: The truth is that not only can nonverbal people understand what's going on around them, but in many cases, they're also highly intelligent. Don't fall into the trap of thinking that just because someone can't answer you, you should ignore them. Instead,

talk to them like you would talk to anyone else. Show them the respect they deserve.

- **People with autism learn slower than their peers**: While it is true that some people with ASD do take longer to learn something new, others can learn a new skill much faster than their neurotypical counterparts. Just as every person has their strengths and weaknesses, the same applies to people with ASD. Never expect all people with ASD to be the same.

- **People with autism are zoned out of life**: Many people with autism have repeated behaviors that might make it seem like they are living in their own worlds. This is even more the case when they struggle to maintain eye contact with someone else. Remember that people with autism's brains work differently from their neurotypical peers, so they may also view the world differently. Imagine yourself in a different country where you don't understand the local language or culture. This is how people with autism often feel. There are many times when they are living in a world that they don't understand or are surrounded by people who think differently than they do. Their repeated behaviors are simply a way for them to cope with what they're experiencing and calm themselves down.

- **All people with autism are the same**: If you want to question this stereotype, simply ask yourself: Are all people with diabetes the same? Or are all the people living in the United States the same? The answer is no. So, how can everyone with autism be the same? Sure, there are many symptoms that different people with autism will experience in similar ways, but the same goes for most other disorders or illnesses.

- **People with autism can't achieve greatness**: You can take this stereotype, write it down on a piece of paper, crumple it up, and throw it in the trash. This is absolute rubbish. You'll find people with autism everywhere. They are doctors, teachers, actors, or whatever you want them to be. Don't you believe me? Think of the famous physicist Albert Einstein. He had what is now believed to be autism. The same goes for inventor Sir Isaac Newton and naturalist Charles Darwin. The famous actor Anthony Hopkins was diagnosed with Asperger's syndrome as a child. Entrepreneur Elon Musk is also open about his Asperger's diagnosis. The inventor of Microsoft, Bill Gates, is widely assumed to have ASD. Even the comedian Jerry

Seinfield is open about being on the spectrum. The list goes on and proves that just because someone has ASD, it doesn't mean success isn't waiting for them in their future.

- **Autism is becoming more common**: There aren't more people with autism walking on the earth now than there were 100 years ago. Medical professionals have just become better at diagnosing the condition due to the extensive research that is constantly done on it. In the past, a person had to basically have every single symptom before a diagnosis was made. Now, there's a much better understanding of the different types of autism. As a result, more people are diagnosed and get the treatment they need.

- **People with autism don't want friends**: Just because their condition makes it more difficult for them to interact with others, form relationships, and act in a way that's socially acceptable, doesn't mean they don't want to have friends in their lives. In fact, if you make the effort to understand them and build a relationship on their terms, you may find them to be extremely good and loyal friends.

- **People with autism are aggressive**: Just like any other person may have an outburst from time to time, so can people with autism. These outbursts are usually the result of a specific trigger, such as loud noises, unwanted physical contact, frustration with either not being understood or not understanding the situation they're in, being bullied, and experiencing anxiety and stress. Many of these triggers are things that would upset neurotypical people as well. Some people with autism might not know how to verbally express their frustrations or anger, and as a result, reacting physically might be the only way they can do it.

- **People with autism look the same**: How many times have you heard someone say something like, "That person looks autistic." There is no way that autism can affect a person's physical appearance. As I've mentioned, autism affects how a person's brain works, not how they look.

- **People with autism are emotionless**: Just because someone with autism may not always be able to identify and understand the emotions of others, it doesn't mean they don't feel emotions. In fact, people with ASD experience the exact same emotions as their neurotypical peers, but they might show these emotions in a different way. Many people with ASD also internalize their emotions, and when they don't show them, they are deemed to be emotionless.

EFFECTS OF AUTISM SPECTRUM DISORDER

Children with ASD will develop at a different rate than neurotypical children and may not gain their skills in the typical developmental order. Where neurotypical children will start to show verbal skills by saying a few words before they're one year old, a few phrases before they're two, and short sentences by the age of three—children with ASD won't follow the same route. Many of them are able to say some words by one year, but then either lose this skill or only learn a new word or two in the following months. Some people with ASD never go beyond saying only a few words and will stay nonverbal their entire lives.

Due to the overgrowth in their brains during the first year, many children with ASD will appear to have typical development, with their skills regressing after one year of age and their autism becoming clear at about two years.

In the next two chapters, we will look at the effects of autism in more detail.

For now, let's focus on four of the most obvious differences between children with ASD and their neurotypical peers:

- **Interaction**: Children with ASD often interact with others in a different way than neurotypical children would. They might not respond to their names, smile when others smile at them, make eye contact, or pick up on others' facial expressions. Instead of pointing at something they want, they might lead their parents or caregivers by the hand to the object they want. They might also not look at something their parents are pointing at; for example, if their parents point at a picture of a cat, they may focus on a tree in the background of the picture. All of these can severely affect their ability to develop language skills.

- **Communication**: As mentioned above, the development of verbal skills may be vastly different in children with autism than in their neurotypical peers. This can result in them not being able to understand what you're saying to them or to tell you what they're thinking, feeling, or wanting. This can also cause severe frustration for these children when they're expected to play with other children. Due to their challenges in communicating, these children may resort to tantrums or other behavioral issues as they don't know how else they can communicate with others.

- **High-level skills**: Children with autism may struggle with daily tasks such as prioritizing things, coping with change, paying attention, being organized, and managing emotions. This, combined with their different development of verbal skills, can make it difficult for these children to learn and show others what they've learned. They may have an excellent understanding of math but find it difficult to show others that they can do it. Children with high-functioning ASD such as Asperger's may cope in mainstream schools and will be able to understand their work well, but they might struggle with completing their school tasks due to their struggles with prioritizing. Remember, people with Asperger's are, in general, highly intelligent but may still struggle with functioning at school.

- **Attention to detail**: Children with ASD often have extreme attention to detail. They may notice small things that their neurotypical peers would look past and may learn basic concepts such as letters, numbers, and shapes much easier. However, due to this hyperfocus on smaller details, they might struggle to see the "bigger picture." For example, they might notice every small part of a picture, such as a dog, a tree, red apples in the tree, pink flowers on the grass, and small white clouds in the blue sky, but they can't put it together to understand that the picture that they are looking at is of a dog sitting under an apple tree.

Understanding the basics and most common ways ASD can affect your child lays the important foundation to helping them through the challenges they may face. Now, let's delve deeper into the potential effects ASD can have on your child.

2

HOW AUTISM AFFECTS YOUR CHILD

A round one in every 150 children around the world is affected by ASD (Obinna, 2016). While many children with mild forms of ASD, such as Asperger's, will be able to cope relatively well, others with severe CDD may have lifelong struggles with fitting in or adapting to the challenges in their lives.

No matter what type of ASD your child may have, it's important to understand how it may affect your child. Having this knowledge will help you prepare for the difficulties your child might face so that you can help them overcome them. To help you with this, we will now go in-depth into how ASD may affect your child in different areas of their lives, including developmental skills, social skills, learning, and communication skills.

THE IMPACT OF AUTISM DIAGNOSIS ON YOU AND YOUR CHILD

Let's first look at the impact an autism diagnosis can have, not only on you but also on your child. It can be heartbreaking as a parent to hear that your child has a lifelong condition with no cure. This can make it difficult for you to imagine a life where your child will grow up to become an independent adult, or to even achieve any form of success in their futures. As much as this might be extra difficult for those with severe CDD, many people with ASD have been able to successfully integrate into society and achieve top honors in their respective fields.

The key here is not to let your child's diagnosis determine their outcomes in life. The earlier you intervene, find ways to help your child, and teach them the skills their ASD might cause them to lack, the brighter your little one's future can be. Always remember that there is hope.

Early intervention can help your child improve their social and communication skills at a time when these skills start to excel in neurotypical children. It can help prevent specific problematic and even harmful behaviors in your child from becoming habits. It is even believed that early intervention can reduce a child's symptoms, which can play a big role in them gaining independence as adults.

Getting an early diagnosis and starting treatment can also benefit you as a parent. It will enable you to learn about their condition and give you enough time to test out the various forms of treatment available until you find the best fit for your child's individual needs. All of these lay the foundation for improved outcomes, not just for your child but also for you.

AUTISM IN BOYS VERSUS GIRLS

Boys are four times more likely to be diagnosed with ASD than girls (Butter, 2017); however, this doesn't necessarily mean that boys are more likely to have this condition than girls. Many researchers believe that even though the symptoms will be similar between the two genders, girls with autism tend to be quieter, can imitate social behaviors better, and have better control over their emotions. In general, they mask the symptoms of ASD more successfully. As a result, ASD can appear to be more apparent in boys than in girls, and the parents of boys are more likely to seek medical advice and get the diagnosis.

AUTISTIC BEHAVIORAL PATTERNS

Depending on the severity of your child's ASD, they may have many different behavioral patterns that can cause you to get frustrated and may even be harmful to your child. Let's take a brief look at these typical behaviors:

- **Stimming**: This happens when your child has specific behaviors that they repeat over and over. You might not understand why they're doing this, but it's usually a form of self-soothing.
- **Routines and rituals**: Children with ASD typically thrive in a predictable environment. As a result, they may be highly upset when you change their routines. Even something as small as driving a different route to their school can be so upsetting that they may have a meltdown.
- **Transitions**: If any child enjoys a certain activity, they may have difficulty moving on to another activity. This can be even more so when the child has ASD.
- **Sensory sensitivities**: Children with ASD often have challenges when it comes to using their senses; for example, they might love the feel of a certain object but don't want to come close to

another object made from a different material or that has a different texture.

- **Sensory overload**: Many children with ASD have great difficulty coping when too much is going on around them. This can be something like being in a noisy place or having a bright light on in a room.
- **Unrealistic expectations**: Most children can get extremely frustrated when they want to do something that they don't have the necessary skills for yet. This is even more so in children with ASD, which can result in extreme meltdowns.
- **Narrowed focus and interests**: Children with ASD often fixate on a specific object or have limited interests; for example, they may only want to play with a single toy over and over. This can also go over to their eating habits, as they might only want to eat the same food every day and get so extreme that they'll refuse to eat altogether if they don't get the food they want.
- **Tiredness**: Children with ASD often have difficulty falling and staying asleep. If your child isn't getting proper sleep, it can cause extremely challenging behaviors.

- **Discomfort or pain**: It often happens that children with ASD complain more of pain or can be completely thrown by little discomforts; for example, the feeling of the material of their shirts against their skin can be so overwhelming that they're unable to focus on anything else. Be careful of dismissing your child's pain complaints as simply a symptom of their ASD. They might have hurt themselves without your knowledge and are unable to tell you about this injury.

- **Other conditions**: Children with ASD are more likely to suffer from other conditions, such as ADHD, epilepsy, and mood disorders. This can make it even more difficult for your child to control their behavior. If you ever suspect your child may have another condition, discuss this with their doctor. Your child might need more intensive treatment to help them (and you) cope.

Now that we've discussed the basics of the typical behavioral patterns many children with ASD show, let's take a deeper look into some of these to help you better understand your child and know what you should try to ignore and when you should take action.

STIMMING IN CHILDREN WITH AUTISM

As I've mentioned, stimming is repetitive sounds or movements that many children with ASD make to soothe or stimulate themselves. Some of the most common forms of stimming in children with ASD include flapping their hands or rocking their bodies back and forth.

While many people will have some forms of repetitive behaviors, such as fidgeting with their hands when they're nervous or tapping with their feet, these aren't necessarily the same as stimming. The golden rule that is generally accepted to determine if someone has stimming or just a repetitive behavioral habit is whether this behavior is socially acceptable or not.

In many cases, the stims of people with ASD aren't easily accepted in social circumstances. If you're in a busy store and someone is biting their nails or continuously twirling their hair, chances are no one is paying attention to them. But if someone with ASD starts spinning around in circles or flapping their hands uncontrollably, it will likely be frowned upon.

Some of the most common stims of people with ASD include

- hand flapping
- finger licking
- lining up objects
- rocking their bodies
- repeated speech
- repeating the words of someone else, known as echolalia
- pacing up and down
- humming
- hard blinking
- flicking switches
- opening and closing doors
- tapping on surfaces
- covering and uncovering their ears

In most cases, these stims are harmless and will actually help the child with ASD cope with their feelings and what's going on around them. They may stim when they're upset and frustrated or when they're happy and excited. If your child's stims don't cause them any harm, it's best to leave them alone, as this will help them to diffuse when they're feeling overstimulated.

However, when your child's stims can be potentially harmful, you'll have to think of ways to help them manage their stims more effectively. Some of these stims can include

- excessive scratching themselves.
- biting their nails to the extent where they're bleeding.
- bang their heads.
- biting their hands or other body parts.
- clapping their ears.
- hitting themselves.

It's not always easy to manage stimming and change certain behaviors, especially if these stims are causing the child some sort of relief from feeling overstimulated. Many people make the mistake of punishing a child with ASD for their stims, but this won't help the situation. In fact, it can make the stimming worse.

To help a child manage their stims, it's best to try and find the source of them. Pay close attention to what's happening to or around your child when they do certain stims. If they bang their heads every time they hear loud noises, you can help them manage these stims by keeping them in a quiet environment or even getting them noise-canceling headphones. If your child scratches themselves when the lights are on in their room, look at options where you can dim the light.

Always remember that stimming isn't a sign of bad behavior. It's a tool they use to cope.

Children with ADHD often also have a degree of stimming, such as fidgeting with their hands or singing a song while they do schoolwork. However, with these children, the stimming will actually help them to focus on the task they are busy with and avoid distractions.

AUTISM AND A CHILD'S DEVELOPMENTAL SKILLS

Children with ASD develop differently from their neurotypical peers. As I've explained, this is largely due to the overgrowth of their brains, which typically happens during the first year of their lives, followed by extremely slow or even arrested growth thereafter.

Some of the first developmental milestones that they might miss are sitting up and social smiles. Later on, the missed milestones can include walking, verbal skills, social and emotional abilities, and with some children, learning difficulties.

It is often missed milestones that will lead your child's doctor to start evaluating them for ASD.

However, this can be a lot more complicated than it appears to be, due to these reasons:

- Many children with ASD will reach their early milestones on time or even earlier than their neurotypical peers, but then slow down with their development.
- Some children with ASD appear to develop certain important skills but are unable to use these skills effectively.
- Some children with ASD may develop exceptional skills—often called "splinter skills" —which aren't useful in their daily lives.
- Some children with ASD, especially girls, are often able to mask their symptoms to such an extent that the diagnosis comes very late or sometimes not at all.

Since there is no blood test that can confirm an ASD diagnosis, medical specialists and parents are often reluctant to make a diagnosis or even get a child diagnosed. The Centers for Disease Control and Prevention recommend that if a child struggles to perform the following tasks by the age of three, an evaluation should be done (Rudy, 2022a):

- Can't work basic toys, such as simple puzzles and turning handles.
- Can't speak in short sentences.
- Doesn't understand basic instructions.
- Can't play pretend.
- Doesn't want to play with other children.
- Only want to play with a single toy.
- Doesn't make eye contact.
- Loses skills they used to have.

AUTISM AND A CHILD'S LEARNING SKILLS

Even though many children with mild ASD such as Asperger's are regarded as highly intelligent, many of them struggle with learning in the typical ways most mainstream schools expect children to do. This can result in them not performing to the best of their abilities at school, or even failing to thrive in mainstream schools.

However, instead of looking at your child's different ways of thinking and learning as difficulties, you can choose to see these as strengths. If you adapt your child's work according to their stretches, they may surprise you with how easily they are able to learn new concepts and skills.

If your child has seen an occupational therapist as part of their evaluation and diagnosis, this specialist has likely done a developmental assessment on your child. These tests measure your child's abilities in areas that include nonverbal thinking, language, communication, movement, and social skills. Your child's therapist will discuss the outcome of this test with you. Therefore, you can determine what your child's strengths are. This specialist will likely be able to guide you with specific exercises and practices you can introduce to help your child.

Many children with ASD benefit from visual thinking and learning. This is due to their exceptional attention to detail and ability to focus on specific aspects of a picture rather than the whole or bigger picture. For these children, visual information is easier to understand and remember than hearing or speaking information. It can help them to process the information much more effectively and, over time, comprehend what behaviors are deemed inappropriate and choose a more acceptable way to behave or respond.

Help your child by thinking of ways you can present their learning work in a visual manner.

Here are some examples of how you can do it, but always adapt it according to your child's age and needs:

- Put visual reminders around your house of the work your child needs to learn.
- Make an activity board of your child doing different activities. This can help remind them that they don't have to repeat the same activity or play with the same toy over and over.
- If they need to learn a new skill, put pictures up of the different steps they need to take.

AUTISM AND A CHILD'S SOCIAL SKILLS

Many children with ASD struggle with social skills. They will behave in ways that are seen as socially inappropriate or, if they're verbal, say things that others might consider rude. Always remember that your child's social behavior might seem odd not because there's something wrong with them, but because they have a different way of socializing that neurotypical people often struggle to understand.

There are many different ways in which a child with ASD might behave in a manner that is against social norms.

Some of the most common ways include

- not making eye contact.
- difficulty debating.
- not seeing any purpose to small talk.
- struggling with the concept of sarcasm.
- holding a conversation where the use of verbal and nonverbal cues is expected.

People with ASD also often struggle with empathy and understanding the feelings of others. This can lead to neurotypical people also lacking empathy when they're interacting with someone with ASD. This is similar to how cultural norms differ and someone from one culture may struggle to understand another person with a different cultural background. Since they don't understand each other's cultures, they can struggle to understand each other's behaviors.

The same goes for interactions between people with ASD and their neurotypical peers. They often don't understand each other, and as a result, there may be a lack of empathy coming from both parties involved. Empathy goes both ways, and if the neurotypical person makes more of an effort to understand why a child with ASD behaves in certain ways, the interaction between them will likely improve.

The more you show your child that you're trying to understand their mannerisms and quirks, if you will, the more your child will open up to you and want to accept and understand the advice you're giving them. We will discuss ways in which you can help your child develop their social skills in greater detail in Chapter 5.

AUTISM AND COMMUNICATION SKILLS

Apart from the difficulties children with ASD can have when it comes to interacting with others, they may also lack the necessary communication skills. Children with severe ASD may be nonverbal, with only a handful of people—such as their parents or carers—understanding what they're trying to say. They may even struggle to respond when others are calling their names.

Always remember that just as frustrating as it can be for you to try to communicate with your nonverbal child, it will most likely be even more frustrating for them. As much as you may get upset, try your best to stay calm. The more negatively you react to their lack of communication, the more your child will struggle to communicate with you.

Even children with developed language skills, such as those with Asperger's, may struggle with their communication skills. Here, it isn't due to a lack of verbal skills but rather to their having difficulty understanding nonverbal or indirect cues. An example of this is when the child talks about something that they're highly interested in. They might not realize that the person they're talking with has lost interest in the topic. This can then result in them rambling on, with the other person getting irritated to the point where they might shut the child up.

Make sure you're direct in your communication with your child. Tell them when you've heard enough by saying something like, "I love how interested you are in this topic, but do you think we can talk about it a bit later again?"

Also, never make assumptions when your child tells you something that you're not sure you're understanding correctly. This can lead to a lot of frustration for your child. Instead, ask them if you understand what they're saying; for example, "I think you're saying that you want to have an apple. Am I correct?" If you don't understand your child, they will know that, at the very least, you're trying to. Asking them to try to explain again what they want will be less frustrating for them than assuming you know what they want and giving them the wrong thing.

SENSORY DIFFICULTIES FOR NEURODIVERGENT CHILDREN

Many children with ASD struggle with sensory processing. This happens when their senses are either overly or underly sensitive. This can be a difficult one for parents to juggle, as a sense that might be under-sensitive (hyposensitive) today, can be over-sensitive (hypersensitive tomorrow. So, for example, the textures in their food that they're happy to eat one day might be too much for them the very next.

Let's look at the different senses and how they can affect your child during phases of hyposensitivity and hypersensitivity.

Sight

This refers to everything your child sees.

If your child is under-sensitive

- things may look very dark.
- they might not see some of the features on objects.
- their vision can seem blurred.
- they may have poor depth perception, resulting in them struggling to throw or catch a ball or appear to be clumsy.

If your child is over-sensitive

- their vision can seem distorted; for example, bright lights can look like they are jumping around.
- they may only see parts of a picture.
- they can only focus on looking at small things.
- they may be so sensitive to light that they can't fall asleep.

You can help your child adjust to their daily needs by installing dimmers on your light switches, getting them sunglasses, putting blackout curtains in their bedroom, and providing them with a workspace with divides on both sides to avoid any visual distractions.

Sound

This refers to everything your child hears.

If your child is under-sensitive

- they may temporarily lose hearing in one ear.
- they might not hear specific sounds.
- they may have difficulty coping in noisy environments or with loud noises.

If your child is over-sensitive

- noise may seem muddled or distorted.
- they may hear background noise clearly.
- they may struggle with cutting out background noise.

Help your child explain to others why their hearing might seem bad at times. Keep the doors and windows closed to reduce background noise. Ensure they are well-prepared before they need to visit noisy places, and if possible, get them noise-canceling headphones or earphones playing music. Try to create a workstation for them that is as far away from windows and doors as possible.

Smell

This refers to what your child can smell.

If your child is under-sensitive

- they may lose their sense of smell temporarily.
- they may want to lick things to try to understand what they would smell like.

If your child is over-sensitive

- smells can completely overpower them, which can result in them not being willing to have a bowel movement.
- they might have extreme dislikes of certain toiletries, perfumes, or even foods.

You can help your child by sticking to toiletries and cleaning products that are unscented. Figure out what smells your child can generally tolerate and keep toiletries in these scents on hand to help them cope with smells they can't handle. Avoid wearing perfumes or using air fresheners in your home.

Taste

This refers to everything your child can taste, including the textures of food.

If your child is under-sensitive

- they want to eat extremely spicy food.
- they may put non-edible things in their mouth, such as stones, soil, grass, metal, or even feces.

If your child is over-sensitive

- they might refuse to eat food with strong flavors.
- they may not want to eat foods with different textures.

This can be difficult to manage if your child has days of under-sensitivity, followed by over-sensitive days. Play it day by day and stick to making their food bland. If they have an under-sensitive day, they can always put hot sauce on their food, but you can't take spice out of their food on an over-sensitive day. If they have difficulty eating textures, give them smooth foods, such as mashed potatoes. Try to include as much variety in their diet as possible so that they get the nutrients, vitamins, and minerals they need.

Touch

This refers to how things feel for them.

If your child is under-sensitive

- they may hold others or animals too tight.
- they might not feel when they have food in their mouth.
- they may have an exceptionally high pain threshold.

- they enjoy heavy objects on them, such as weighted blankets.
- they chew on everything, including their clothes.
- they may hurt themself.

If your child is over-sensitive

- any form of touch can feel like a stabbing pain.
- they may hate wearing shoes.
- their head can be so sensitive that they refuse to brush their hair.
- they might struggle with different textures.
- they may only want to wear certain types of material.

You can help by offering them alternatives, such as keeping foods or fruits with textures they can usually tolerate in the kitchen. Warn them before you're going to touch them, and always approach them from the front in case they're overly sensitive. Always remember that a hug might be painful for them instead of comforting. Gradually introduce new textures or materials, and never force them to wear something they don't want to. They aren't being difficult; some materials are literally hurting their skin. Turn their clothes inside out so that there are no seams or tags that might scratch them.

Balance

This refers to the position of their heads and their vestibular system.

If your child is under-sensitive

- they constantly need to stim, such as rocking their bodies or spinning around in circles.

If your child is over-sensitive

- they may struggle in taking part in sport.
- they may struggle to control their movements.
- they might get car sick easily.
- they may have difficulty with any activity that requires them to lift their feet off the ground.

Help them improve their vestibular system through activities such as riding on a rocking horse or a swing, seesaws, or roundabouts. On days of oversensitivity, you can break down their tasks into manageable chunks and use visual cues to help them through the activity.

Body awareness

This refers to them understanding how their bodies move.

If your child is under-sensitive

- they may struggle with judging distance and, as a result, stand too close to others.
- find it difficult to avoid obstacles when they walk.

They may bump into others.

If your child is over-sensitive

- they may have difficulty with fine motor skills.
- they might move their entire body (not just their necks) to look at something.

You can help them by moving all the furniture to the edges of rooms and avoiding using a coffee table in the middle of the living room. Weighted blankets can help them while they're sleeping. You can teach them the "arm's length" rule and that they should always be able to put their arms out around them when they stand close to others. Fine motor skill development will help them on days when they're oversensitive.

Now that you have a good understanding of the overall struggles children with ASD may face, let's look at the different life stages and how your child may be affected.

3

THE CHALLENGES OF DIFFERENT LIFE STAGES

In every stage of your child's life, their ASD may affect them in different ways. As the parent of a child with ASD, I've found it extremely valuable to be prepared for what might come your way. This way, none of the typical behaviors your child might have during these different life stages will surprise you, and you will know what you should do and how you can help them.

Always remember: The more you help your child, the easier they will be able to deal with their symptoms, and the bigger chance you'll have of raising a child who can grow into an independent adult. To help you through this, we will now explore the different stages of a child's life, from babyhood to toddlerhood, being a young child, and being a teenager. Then, I'll give you my top 10 suggestions on things you can focus on to help your child become more independent.

Before we get into all of this, let's start out by discussing the common challenges many people with ASD face on a daily basis.

COMMON CHALLENGES PEOPLE WITH AUTISM FACE

Apart from social, cognitive, verbal, and behavioral issues your child might have, many children with ASD also often struggle with various mental health conditions, including anxiety disorder, depression, and ADHD. It is believed that around seven out of ten people with ASD will also have another mental health condition at some point in their lives (*Autism and mental health*, n.d.).

Although the reasons for this can be very dependent on every person's personality, circumstances, and the severity of their ASD, some of the most common causes can include:

- Inability to fit in.
- Not understanding the world.
- Being easily distracted.
- May face more stigma and discrimination.

- Not getting support.

Let's look at these three conditions, how they often overlap with ASD, and how you can help your child.

Anxiety Disorder

Most people experience some degree of anxiety in their lives; the same is true for children living with ASD. However, when they experience excessive worries or fears that impact their ability to live, and they continue for more than six months, your child might have an anxiety disorder. This is extremely common among people with ASD: studies have shown that up to 84% of people with ASD also meet the criteria for anxiety disorders (*Common challenges*, 2022).

Even though there are many different forms of anxiety disorders, the most common ones are:

- **Generalized anxiety disorder**: This happens when your child is experiencing fears and worries over a variety of aspects of their lives. They can also have anxiety over nothing specific. It can include having phobias about germs or even different textures and foods.
- **Social anxiety**: This is often the case in people with ASD. Since they don't always understand social cues, and they often lack the skills to

interact with others, they may become exceptionally fearful of being around other people, particularly people they don't know.

- **Separation anxiety**: This happens when a child has extreme fears about leaving their parents, even if only for a few minutes. This often happens in children that are nonverbal, as, in many cases, their parents are the only people that can understand their unique ways of communicating.
- **Post-traumatic stress disorder (PTSD)**: If your child experienced some degree of trauma, they might struggle with PTSD later in life. This trauma can include being exposed to violence or abuse or having been injured. It can set in years after the trauma.

Even though anxiety is quite common among those with ASD, it often goes undiagnosed. This is particularly the case with nonverbal people, as they lack the ability to voice their fears and concerns. In a person with ASD, anxiety usually manifest in the follow ways:

- phobias
- excessive worry
- obsessive-compulsive behavior
- avoidance behaviors

- hypervigilance
- controlling behaviors
- meltdowns

Depression

Every person has times in their lives when they experience excessive sadness. However, when these feelings continue for a few weeks, and it affects their daily life, your child might be suffering from the mood disorder depression. It is believed that depression affects around half of all people with ASD at some point in their lives (*Depression*, n.d.).

There are many reasons why those with ASD can be more likely to suffer from depression. These can include

- not understanding emotions (in themselves or others).
- lack of support.
- difficulty navigating social situations.
- not being understood or accepted by their neurotypical peers.

Depression is a treatable condition; however, if your child is nonverbal, you might not necessarily become aware of their condition until they're really struggling. Signs that your child might be depressed can include

- continuous low moods.
- not having hope for the future.
- changes in appetite.
- lack of energy.
- not wanting to see people.
- increased repetitive behaviors.
- more meltdowns.
- not showing interest in things they used to enjoy.
- suicidal ideation.

If your child ever shows any signs of anxiety or depression, it's important that you mention this to their doctor. If necessary, the doctor can prescribe medication, such as antidepressants and antianxiety pills, that can help your child manage their symptoms.

ADHD

About half of people with ASD will also show signs of ADHD (*ADHD and Autism Spectrum Disorder*, n.d.). These are both neurodevelopmental disorders that can affect a child in very similar ways (although the symptoms of ASD are usually much more severe).

Let's look at some of the different behaviors of ADHD and ASD, and how they often correlate with each other.

Symptoms of ADHD	Symptoms of ASD
Difficulty sitting still.	Have specific stimmings.
Difficulty focusing on one activity.	Can be overfocused on an activity.
Easily distracted.	Easily distracted by sensory sensitivities.
Difficulty to complete a task before moving to the next.	Difficulty shifting their attention to the next task.
Can fixate on something and have hyperfocus.	Can become overly attached to an item and only want to play with one toy.
Can be very impulsive.	Can be very inflexible, especially when it comes to their routines.

If your child shows signs of ADHD on top of their ASD, it's best to consult with their doctor. There are various treatment options available for ADHD, which can make dealing with these symptoms a lot easier.

AUTISM IN BABYHOOD

As I've mentioned, some children may show signs of ASD before their first birthday. Even though this might be the case for all children with this condition, some children might show the first signs by around six months of age. This is when the child still doesn't smile or show any facial expressions.

By nine months, more signs are usually visible. These will include

- not making eye contact with anyone, or even only making limited eye contact.
- don't make cooing sounds in reaction to stimulation.
- not sharing social smiles with their parents.

By the child's first birthday, more signs can be visible when a child

- may not reach for or point to things.
- may not wave.
- may not respond to their names.
- may not babble.

Always remember that many children will show typical development during the phase of brain overgrowth until they turn one year old. After that, once the brain's development slows down or even arrests, more signs of ASD are usually seen.

AUTISM IN TODDLERS

Toddlerhood is often the stage at which children are diagnosed with ASD. The differences between neurotypical children and those with ASD become a lot more apparent, especially when their neurotypical peers start to reach one milestone after another.

Since this is such an important stage in developmental differences that can lead to an early diagnosis, let's first look at the typical signs of ASD in children between the ages of one year (12 months) and 18 months:

- Avoid eye contact with new faces.
- Lack of interest in social interaction, including reluctance to be cuddled or affectionate.
- Difficulty pointing to objects
- Difficulty responding to their own names.
- Limited vocabulary and difficulty expressing needs or desires.
- Lack of interest in seeking help or engaging in baby talk with others.

Many of these symptoms will likely continue past the age of 18 months, with three more signs, often seen in young children that

1. will either not walk or only walk on their toes.
2. may get upset by certain smells, tastes, or sounds.
3. may start repetitive movements.

The older a child gets, the easier it can be to identify potential symptoms that may be associated with ASD. A good example of this is not walking by the age of 18 months or only saying a few, limited words by this age. However, unless you're fully aware that this can indicate a problem like ASD, these symptoms are often missed by parents and caregivers.

Most parents only seek out an evaluation for their children between the ages of two and three years. Let's look at typical symptoms to expect at this time:

- Can't speak or still only say a few words.
- Plays differently to other children, such as by lining up their toys instead of playing with them, or only playing with one specific toy.
- Difficulty following simple instructions.
- Make very limited gestures, if any.
- Don't enjoy being with other children.
- Struggle to make friends.
- Difficulty understanding simple concepts (or showing you that they understand them).
- Struggle to explain how they're feeling.
- Difficulty understanding the feelings of others.
- Can come across as oppositional.
- Thrives under set routines.
- Gets extremely upset when a routine is changed or interrupted.

- Keen interest in very specific things.
- Continuously talk about the things they're interested in (if they are verbal).

Even though most children are diagnosed during toddlerhood, some may only be evaluated when they start formal schooling. This is usually when teachers pick up on differences in your child.

AUTISM IN YOUNG CHILDREN

Signs of autism can be very obvious by the time your child reaches school-going age. Again, this does depend on the severity of your child's ASD. Many children with Asperger's syndrome can still go undiagnosed, especially when enough effort has been made to help them develop their communication and social skills.

Let's look at typical behaviors of children in this age group:

- Saying less than 15 words.
- When they seem confused by everyday items or events.
- Not responding to their name.
- Not walking, or still walking only on their toes.
- Not imitating actions or words.
- Inability to push a wheeled toy.

- Not following simple instructions.
- Prefer spending time alone.
- Having stimmings.
- Wanting to have strict routines.
- Not enjoying physical contact.
- Not understanding the thoughts and feelings of others.
- Losing skills they used to have.

Even though it's always best to get your child diagnosed as young as possible for the treatment options to be as effective as possible, it's never too late. If you only notice signs of ASD in your child once they start to attend mainstream school, they will still greatly benefit from the treatment that will be available once a diagnosis has been made.

AUTISM IN TEENAGERS AND ADOLESCENTS

When it comes to teenagers with ASD, I found it easiest to divide their potential symptoms into different categories. This way, it's easier to understand what you can look out for in your child. Let's first look at verbal communication in teenagers with ASD:

- May struggle taking turns in conversations.
- Talk excessively about things that interest them.

- Have difficulty understanding sarcasm and figures of speech.
- May sound different from their neurotypical peers; for example, they may speak loudly without variation in tone or with a strange accent.
- Have good vocabularies.
- Use formal language.
- Have difficulty following more than two steps in an instruction.

When it comes to nonverbal communication in teenagers with ASD, the symptoms might look vastly different:

- Difficulty reading nonverbal cues from others, such as body language.
- Minimum eye contact with others or avoid it altogether.
- Show fewer emotions.
- Unable to understand the emotions of others.
- Show very limited facial expressions.
- Use only a few gestures to help express themselves.

Next, let's look at symptoms that may come along with how teenagers with ASD may build relationships with others:

- Prefer to spend time alone.
- Insists that others must follow the rules.
- Have difficulty understanding typical social rules.
- Struggle to make new friends.
- Have difficulty relating to other children their age.
- Struggle to adjust their behavior to what is socially acceptable or for specific social situations.

The repetitive behaviors, or stimmings of teenagers with ASD, as well as their interests, can also change as they grow older. Let's look at what is typical at this age:

- Specific interests.
- Behaviors that might seem like compulsions.
- Overly attached to certain objects.
- Can get upset when routines change.
- Specific body movements that soothe them.
- Make repetitive noises.

Apart from these symptoms, eating disorders are common among teenagers with ASD. This can be as a result of anxiety they may experience, bullying due to being different, or sensory sensitivity that makes it difficult for them to eat certain foods.

They may also struggle to cope with the workload in mainstream schools. This can include prioritizing and organizing tasks and managing time. This can result in many teenagers with ASD refusing to go to school or falling victim to being bullied by their peers.

AUTISM AND ADULT INDEPENDENCE

While you're parenting your child through the different life stages, it's important to always try to increase their independence. The more you do this, the greater their independence as adults might be. It is, however, important to be realistic when it comes to teaching independence, as children with severe CDD may not be able to ever be truly independent.

If your child has this type of ASD, take it one day at a time. Never put too much pressure on them or yourself, and remember that the efforts you make will reap rewards, whether these rewards are them gaining independence or just helping make life easier for them.

Over the years, I've tried many different ways to help my son. Some have failed, and some have been extremely effective.

Let's look at my top 10 tips for helping your child gain independence:

- **Improve communication**: If your child struggles with developing language skills or is nonverbal, you can try different techniques to improve their ability to communicate. This can be by using sign language, visual supports which you can find on many applications you can download on a smartphone or a tablet, or getting them a speech output device.
- **Have a visual schedule**: If your child struggles to read or works better with visual cues, you can create a visual schedule for them. This will help them remember the different tasks they can or have to do. In the beginning, you'll probably have to help them complete their tasks. However, the more you stick to this, the more they'll learn to do these tasks by themselves.
- **Help them with self-care skills**: Look at your child's capabilities and introduce small skills gradually to help them take care of themselves. Start small by letting them comb their hair by

themselves. In the beginning, you'll probably have to guide their hands, but eventually, they will learn how to do this. Once they've learned this skill, start the next one, such as brushing their teeth. Remember to include these tasks on your child's visual schedule to remind them.

- **Help them take breaks**: Knowing when you need to take a break from your tasks is an important skill all people should have to avoid burnout. The same goes for people with ASD. Help your child find ways to ask for a break. This can be a break button on their communication device, a picture that indicates a break, or a physical object that they can pick up when they've had enough. You can also identify a space in your home where your child can enjoy their break in peace or go when they feel overwhelmed. This might seem insignificant, but it is an important step in your child's learning to take control of themselves and their environment.

- **Give them a chore**: Even if it's something as simple as putting their dirty clothes in the laundry hamper, they will learn to take responsibility for something. Once your child can do this task easily, introduce another chore. If they struggle to complete an entire chore, break it up into smaller pieces and let them start by only completing one portion of the task. Help your child with prompts if they struggle to complete a task.

- **Help them with money skills**: Every person must learn to deal with money if they have any hopes of living independently. It can be as simple as giving your child a few dollars to buy something at the store. If they don't understand the concept of numbers, add some visuals to the numbers; for example, a ball next to the number one, a duck next to the number two, and so forth. This way they will learn to associate a number with an item, which can help them recognize numbers easier and know what money note they should give for an item that costs a dollar.

- **Teach them about safety**: As with any other child, safety can be a big concern when a child gains more independence. Start with something easy, such as pedestrian safety. Put up visuals around the home to remind them of the specific rules they'll have to follow. Once they become comfortable with one skill, introduce another one. It can also be helpful to give your child an ID card with all the necessary information on it, such as their name, your number, and a brief explanation of their condition. Even if they never leave the house without you, get them into the habit of always making sure they have their card with them.

- **Teach them something fun**: Look at the things that your child is extremely interested in and see if there isn't an activity that connects to this interest. Having fun while doing something they are interested in will help your child let go of any tension and anxiety they might experience and realize that not everything in life has to be serious.

- **Self-care during adolescence**: It's important that your child can master basic self-care skills before they reach puberty, such as combing their hair or brushing their teeth. This is the time that you'll want to increase your practice of basic hygiene. Use visual aids in the bathroom to remind them what to do: use soap to wash their bodies, identify which body parts should be washed in which order, use shampoo for their hair, put deodorant on, and so forth. It can also be helpful to create a hygiene caddy for your child with everything they might need in it.

- **Look at vocational skills**: As your child grows older, look at specific vocational skills you can teach them. Again, look at your child's interests and capabilities and see if there is a specific skill that they can learn that will help them become more financially independent.

Always remember to only take on as much as your child can handle. There's no point in trying to implement all 10 of these steps at once. Instead, take it one step at a time if you have to, and make sure your child is ready for more before you introduce the next step.

EVERYDAY CHANGES AND HORIZONTAL PLANNING VERSUS LONG-TERM CHANGES AND VERTICAL PLANNING

Understanding what your child is struggling with and what typical symptoms may wait for them in the coming years can help you plan their lives better so that they are more prepared for what may lie ahead. This is where horizontal planning for everyday tasks and vertical planning for long-term tasks come in.

Horizontal Planning

This will help prepare your child for changes in their daily lives and their strict routines. It is inevitable that your child will experience some changes. However, the better they are prepared for these changes, the better they will be able to handle them.

Let's look at some of the daily changes your child might struggle with, known as "horizontal transitions," for example:

- eating new foods
- having visitors
- leaving the house
- going somewhere unfamiliar, such as a doctor
- doing things out of routine
- switching from one activity to the next one

Since many people with ASD have strong visual skills, it can be helpful to use these skills to let them know a change is coming. This will then help them transition easier, as they will have time to prepare themselves for it. If they need to transition to a task that they've done before, show them a photo of them doing this task. If they need to go to a place they've never been before, do a quick online search for pictures of this place.

If your child must see someone, such as a new doctor, and you can't find a recent picture of them online, call the reception beforehand, explain your situation, and ask if they can send you a picture of the doctor. Most people would be willing to accommodate these types of requests, especially since this will make the appointment with the doctor go a lot smoother if your child is prepared.

Vertical Planning

This is the type of planning you'll have to do to help your child cope with long-term changes. You might have to move to a different town, or they'll have to transition to a different school to further their education. These transitions can cause a lot of stress and anxiety in any child, but especially those with ASD, as they will likely struggle more with any unknown factors.

I've found the Five-Point-Vertical Plan to be highly effective in planning how you can make these types of changes easier for your child. Let's look at the five steps:

1. **Get all the information**: Start out by considering the change that is about to happen. When is it going to happen? Where will this change take place? Will there be anyone they know going through this transition with them? How has your child dealt with similar changes in the past? What helped them to deal with these transitions?

2. **Make a plan**: Set an appointment with the people who will help your child through this change. Ask them if there's anything they'd like you to tell your child to prepare them? Tell them anything you think they need to know and understand about your child.

3. **Get the supports ready**: This can be anything from pictures, stories, sensory supports, or even a short movie that you can make to help them anticipate what will happen. Make it as interesting as you can.

4. **Implement the plan**: Use your supports to explain to your child exactly what will happen, why it will happen, when it will happen, where it will happen, and how it will happen. If your child has a specific object that helps them calm down, let them hold it while you explain the change to them. Repeat this as often as you have to get your child calm about the change that's taking place.

5. **Evaluate**: Once the change has happened, look at your plan and make notes of what worked, what didn't work, and what you think would be better in the future. Keep these notes to remind yourself the next time you need to do vertical planning to help your child.

One of the biggest breakthroughs in my challenges helping my son was the day I discovered dialectical behavior therapy. In the next chapter, I will explain how this type of therapy and its four pillars—mindfulness, interpersonal effectiveness, distress tolerance, and emotional regulation—can change the way you parent your child for the better.

4

PRACTICAL DIALECTICAL BEHAVIOR THERAPY FOR AUTISM

While I was trying to find ways to help my son, I explored many different types of therapy. We tried applied behavior analysis, cognitive behavioral therapy, joint attention therapy, and many more without much success. There were times when I wanted to give up, but every time I looked at my child's innocent face, I knew I had to keep going. I knew I had to find a way to help him.

Eventually, I came across dialectical behavior therapy (DBT) and decided to give it a try. I will admit that, at first, I was extremely skeptical. If none of the other types of therapy brought me the results that I knew my child deserved, why would DBT be any different? Well, I was amazed at how this changed all of our lives. It taught me to be a better parent, accept my child without any judgment, stay calm, and be more mindful of my child's needs. And it helped my child cope with his daily life and manage his symptoms of ASD much more effectively.

Let's take a deeper look at what DBT entails and why it's effective for the treatment of ASD. I will also share some of the exercises I've introduced in our home that have helped my son tremendously.

WHAT IS DIALECTICAL BEHAVIOR THERAPY?

If you haven't heard of DBT before, let me explain what it's all about. It is a form of psychotherapy or talk therapy. It has been designed specifically to help people who experience intense emotions, as is often the case in people with ASD.

Since the word "dialectical" means to act on or combine opposite things or ideas, DBT helps a person accept your reality instead of fighting against it and then change your reaction to this reality. In ASD, it will mean you will learn to accept the diagnosis and symptoms that come with it, but choose to change the behaviors that these symptoms usually result in.

Originally, DBT was designed to treat mental health conditions such as borderline personality disorder (BPD), PTSD, substance use disorder, depression, anxiety, and eating disorders. I think this is probably where my skepticism kicked in; if the treatment that was designed specifically for autism didn't help my son, why would therapy designed for other conditions help my son cope with his ASD?

After doing more research and giving it a lot of thought, I realized that ASD actually shares some characteristics with BPD and many of the other mental health conditions listed above. They are all based on dealing with intense emotions and choosing the wrong behaviors to deal with these feelings. In many of them, interpersonal relationships are problematic, moods are unstable, intense anger is difficult to control, and stress-related paranoia can be debilitating.

DBT is based on accepting your condition and the difficulties that may come with it and choosing to react in better ways instead of fighting your condition and allowing the frustrations that may come with this reality to overcome you and determine your life. DBT is about strict and repeated behaviors that focus on emotional regulation and gaining control of your actions. This fits perfectly with the desire that most people with ASD have to follow strict and predictable routines and rules. Once I came to this realization, I was convinced that we had to give it a try. And, we haven't looked back.

Let's look at some of the benefits we have experienced since we started using DBT to treat ASD:

- Managing emotions helps to navigate the struggles that come with social settings.
- Acceptance of ASD helps to become more aware of the typical red flags that cause disruptive behavior.
- Identifying these red flags helps reduce and avoid unnecessary conflict.
- The structures of DBT therapy bring stability and predictability to an otherwise uncertain world.
- Improved behavior due to DBT practices helps to reduce judgment and boost social relationships.
- These relationships help reduce feelings of self-harm and suicidal ideation.
- Being more self-aware helps to become more aware of sensory needs to reduce and prevent meltdowns.
- The skills taught in DBT help people calm down quicker after a meltdown.

DBT has reminded me again that we are all capable beings, no matter what the diagnosis might be. This new mindset helped to reshape how I viewed my son's symptoms and helped my son realize that, even though certain tasks may be more difficult for him, he can complete them successfully.

HOW DOES IT WORK?

While many other types of therapies place a lot of focus on the reasons for problematic behaviors, DBT is about accepting these behaviors and finding better ways to cope with them. It is built on four pillars: mindfulness, interpersonal effectiveness, distress tolerance, and emotional regulation.

Mindfulness

This practice has been around for centuries, forming the basis of Buddhist meditation. It's about being present in the moment, paying attention only to what you're doing and how you're feeling.

The purpose of being mindful when controlling the symptoms of ASD, is to help your child calm themselves down before they react based on their emotions. It's about carefully considering what they're experiencing and what causes them to feel this way, instead of just blowing up and behaving in a way that makes others upset. It's about accepting themselves and, through this, strengthening their relationships, not just with themselves but also with others. Furthermore, it's about realizing that what they're feeling are just emotions, and if they give it a bit of time, these emotions will subside naturally.

Interpersonal Effectiveness

This is about the relationships your child has, their wants and needs, and the role they play in these. It's about having respect for themselves and others. It is about protecting themselves during difficult times and telling (or showing) others directly what they require and do not require.

The more your child can learn to improve their relationships with others, the more they will be able to break down any limiting beliefs they might have about themselves and the people in their lives. Through mutual respect, they may even learn to be more trusting of others and allow more people into their circle.

Distress Tolerance

Your child (and you) will likely experience difficult emotions at times. These feelings can overwhelm them so much that they may struggle to control themselves. This can result in unbearable situations for both of you and, in severe circumstances, can undo any progress they might've made leading up to the meltdown.

This is why teaching them distress tolerance skills can be so life changing. They are designed to distract your child from the challenging emotions they may have. This can make it easier for them to regulate these emotions and stop them from reacting in an over-the-top manner. They will realize that once they accept themselves and their emotions, they will be able to overcome these challenging times a lot easier and without responding with harmful behaviors.

Emotional Regulation

Tying into distress tolerance, the more your child will be able to regulate their own emotions, the easier they will be able to deal with their symptoms of ASD. Successfully managing emotions is not just about dealing with difficult negative emotions; it's also about learning to control the extreme elation children with ASD can often experience. It's about them constantly being aware they're feeling and deciding what will be the best way to deal with these emotions without reacting in the type of behaviors that may be socially unacceptable. We will discuss this in more detail in the next chapter.

PRACTICAL DBT SKILLS THAT WORK

There are many different DBT exercises that you can do with your child that can help them become more mindful, improve their relationships with others, manage their emotions, and deal with distressing experiences. Depending on the severity of your child's condition, I would suggest you pick one of these exercises that you think your child will be able to do. Once they can easily do one exercise, add another one.

If your child is a visual learner, remember to add this to their visual schedule by taking photos of them doing each exercise and adding this to their schedule. I'll add suggestions with each exercise about how you can make it more visual for your child to learn. Some of the exercises may seem like duplicates, but they can be done at different skill levels; for example, *Square Breathing, Balloon Breath,* and *Hot Chocolate Breath* are all breathing exercises but require different techniques. If your child struggles to do one, then try the other exercise.

Square Breathing

This is one of the most effective DBT skills, despite being extremely basic. Through this, your child will use deep breathing to manage their stress and anxiety. They can do this quickly and, in any environment, to calm themselves down and give them time to consider how they should behave. For example, if they're experiencing sensory under-sensitivity and struggle to cope with the noises they hear, they can use *Square Breathing* to calm down and reduce the effect that these noises will have on them.

Here's how to do it. Let them

- inhale for four counts.
- hold their breath for four counts.
- exhale for four counts.
- hold it for four counts.

In the beginning, I would suggest you use your fingers to show the four counts. As they get used to this breathing technique, you can help them use their own fingers. Over time, let them count on their fingers without help (if possible). This way, they will learn to do this exercise completely by themselves.

Balloon Breath

This breathing technique is ideal when your child is either very young or their condition is severe. In this case, you can let them blow an imaginary balloon (or bubble, if you prefer).

It's easy to do, and another exercise you can help your child with anywhere is:

- Hold your hands together in front of your child's face. Ask them to blow the bubble.
- As they blow, form an imaginary bubble or balloon with your hands.
- If your child makes short, shallow breaths, then only move your hands slightly. If they make deep breaths, make bigger movements with your hands to show them how the bubble is getting bigger. This will help to encourage them to take deeper breaths as their balloon gets bigger.
- Once your child has calmed down, you can ask them to give one last deep, big breath to pop the balloon.

This is an excellent tool to distract your child from whatever is upsetting them and to help them calm down. As they get used to doing this, you can encourage them to use their own hands to make the balloon.

Doing this can also benefit you as the parent, as it will give you a few minutes to calm yourself down as well.

Hot Chocolate Breath

This is another breathing exercise that is easy enough that children of all ages and degrees of ASD can do. Similar to *Balloon Breath*, this exercise requires some visualization and can be done anywhere. In this exercise, your child will pretend they are drinking a cup of hot chocolate.

You can replace this "drink" with your child's favorite beverage, but it should ideally be a warm one:

- Let them hold their hands in front of their faces as if they're holding a cup of hot chocolate. If they can't drink by themselves, you can hold your hands there as if you're helping them to drink.
- Let them visualize smelling the hot chocolate by inhaling deeply through their nose.
- Now, let them blow out through their mouths as if they're trying to cool the hot chocolate with their breath.
- Let your child repeat this a few times until they've calmed down.
- Your child can settle into their own rhythm while doing this exercise, as long as they inhale through their nose and exhale through their mouth.

If they struggle to get this right, you can give them an actual cup of hot chocolate to use to do this until they're able to easily control their breathing. Making the connection between their breathing and hot chocolate (or their favorite beverage) can help them feel more positive about their struggles. Over time, they will realize that no matter how negative their situation may be, they can choose to turn it into something positive.

Accepting the Uncontrollable

This practice is about helping your child accept their condition and anything else they might not have control over. This can be very helpful when they need to deal with difficult symptoms they might experience, as well as normal life events that they have no control over. If they can understand and accept that these events are just a part of life, they can find peace and give themselves permission to let go of certain things. It can also help reduce any anxiety your child might experience.

If your child is verbal, let them name one thing that happened to them every day that they had no control over. Also, name something that happened to you that you couldn't control. This will help your child understand that they aren't the only ones who sometimes lose control.

If your child isn't verbal, let them use a visual aid to explain something that happened to them that they didn't enjoy. It can help to have different pictures available for them so that they can simply pick one up. Do the same by showing them a picture of something that you didn't enjoy on that day.

This exercise ties in well with distress tolerance, as your child will realize that things will happen in their life that they don't want and can't control, but they don't have to allow this to determine how they can and should live. This acceptance can give them the peace they need to choose how they want to respond.

Ride the Wave

This exercise requires some visualization. If your child knows the ocean well, they might be able to do this without much help. Otherwise, you can look online for videos of the waves rolling on the shore. Talk them through the movements of the waves—how they go from something big and scary to getting smaller and smaller until it eventually dissipates.

Help them to understand that the wave is just like their emotions. It can feel overwhelming and scary, but if they just ride it out like a wave, these emotions will get smaller and smaller until they go away naturally.

Put a poster of the ocean or a wave up in their room to remind them of this visualization exercise whenever life gets too much for them to handle. Use online videos or sound clips from the ocean to help them with this. If they're verbal, let them tell themselves something like, "I'm riding the wave." The more they do this visualization, the easier it will get.

Hit Pause

This is a good exercise to do if your child has some verbal skills. This will help them become more aware of what they're feeling and give them the opportunity to calm down before they go into a full meltdown. As a result, their stress and anxieties will feel less overwhelming and debilitating.

To do this, create a specific word or phrase your child can use when they need a break or feel like their emotions are getting the better of them. This can be anything from "stop," "break," "pause," to a short sentence, "Time for a break." When your child says their pause word, everyone in the house must agree that whatever led to this must stop immediately. Whether it was an argument or simply having too much sensory stimulation. Allow everyone time to calm down before you continue the conversation, or give your child a designated space free from sensory overload to help them calm down.

Calm Button

If your child is nonverbal or has severe ASD, you can replace the pause word mentioned above with a *Calm Button*. The idea here is to identify a specific object in your home that calms your child. Rename it as their *Calm Button*. Whenever your child touches this object, it will serve the same purpose as the pause word discussed above.

If your child really struggles with distress tolerance, you can have a few *Calm Buttons* around your home, in their school bag, and also keep one in your car. This will make it easier for your child to reach for the button when they're starting to feel overwhelmed. Gradually teach them to do a few breathing exercises while holding their *Calm Button* to help them regain control over their emotions.

Failing Forward

This exercise is about using your failures as motivation to do better in the future. Instead of punishing or even disciplining your child for the mistakes they've made, you use these mistakes to launch their decisions and growth in the future. This exercise is usually for children with a lower degree of ASD, such as Asperger's. Make sure your child has a good understanding of consequences before you do this with them.

If your child forgets to do a school project because they were fixating on one of the special interests, you might've decided that some sort of punishment is appropriate or even contact the teacher to try to explain the situation and beg them to accept the project late.

If you practice *Failing Forward*, you won't do any of this. Instead, you'll simply ask them how they felt about not handing in their project or how they're going to feel about not getting any mark for that project. Simply leave them with these types of questions and allow this failure to kick-start their internal motivation to finish their schoolwork the next time they have to do a project.

You can adjust this example and the concept of *Failing Forward* to your child's circumstances. It might feel like you're adding more anxiety to your child by letting them think about the consequences of their actions. However, children often experience more anxiety around being punished or disciplined. As a result, you might actually reduce their anxiety by explaining to them that it's up to them to learn the lesson from their failure.

Have a Seat

Many DBT techniques are heavily based on awareness and being mindful, none more so than this exercise. This is basically a child-version of mediation and can be done with any child with some cognitive function. All they need to do is sit quietly and focus on four different aspects, built on the acronym SEAT.

Guide them through this by asking them different questions. They can answer you verbally or keep their answers in their thoughts. As long as they spend time thinking about the questions you're asking, they practice self-awareness. You can also adjust the questions (or add more) according to your child's abilities and circumstances:

- **Sensations**: How does your body feel? Do you have any aches? What do you hear? What can you smell? Can you taste anything?
- **Emotions**: How do you feel? Do you feel happy? What made you sad today? Do you feel worried? What are you afraid of? What made them angry today? What emotion did you feel the most today?
- **Actions**: What do you think you need to do? What do you want to do? Is there a difference between what you want and what you need?

How will you decide what to do? What do you think will happen after you do this?

- **Thoughts**: What are you thinking about? Did you have happy thoughts today? What sad thoughts did you have today? How do you feel about your thoughts? Can you accept your thoughts?

Try to have your child help you do this exercise every day. It will help them understand what's going on in their lives and how they can adjust their actions accordingly. The more they do it, the easier it will become. Eventually, they might even be able to do this quickly by themselves when they experience moments of stress or overwhelm.

Stop Sign

This is a great technique to use while you're teaching your child about distress tolerance and managing their emotions. The purpose of this is to have various moments throughout the day—not just when they're getting emotional—to quickly do a self-check on what they're feeling and what they can do to regain control. Decide on a visual cue that your child can use.

A popular choice is using a stop sign, as this sign literally tells you to stop:

- Post your visual cues at different places around the home and move them around regularly to avoid this becoming too predictable.
- Every time your child sees the visual cue, they should stop whatever they're doing.
- Let them inhale through their nose and exhale through their mouth. These breaths must be as deep as possible.
- Once their breathing settles into a rhythm, let them ask themselves three questions:

What is happening now?
What am I thinking?
How am I feeling?

- Once they've answered these questions, they can continue with their day.

If your child struggles to remember what questions to ask themselves, you can add a reminder to their visual cue. In the beginning, you can ask these questions to your child, but it's ideal that they're able to do this by themselves.

The Silent Sigh

Another calming technique your child can do quickly by themselves is a quick sigh. This helps them to increase the oxygen in their blood quickly and can help to calm them quickly. They can do this anywhere, even in the classroom, for example:

- When they feel like they're getting overwhelmed, let them close their eyes quickly so that they can try to block out the world around them.
- Next, let them sigh by pushing as much air out of their lungs as possible.
- Once they're done sighing, let them inhale deeply through their nose, and then repeat the sigh.

They can do this as many times as they may need until they feel calm enough to continue with the activity that caused them stress. Now, their minds will be clearer, and they may even be able to think of ways to do things that they haven't considered before.

Do the Opposite

Distress tolerance is all about becoming aware of what you're feeling and reacting in the opposite way. For example, if you're angry, you should try to smile. If you're sad, you should try to laugh. As a result of doing this, your child will be distracted from the difficult emotions they're experiencing, and they will learn that even though they're having certain emotions, they can choose to behave in the complete opposite way.

An easy way of doing this is to start by changing their body. If they're sitting down while they're experiencing difficult emotions, let them stand up. If they're walking around, let them stand or sit still. If they're inside, let them go outside.

The more they use their body to react physically in the opposite way, the more they will be able to train their brain to do the same.

Have Fun

It's important that your child has enough time to do something that they really enjoy. Put this in your child's visual schedule. If they're having a difficult time completing tasks they don't enjoy, looking at their schedule will remind them that they will have fun soon.

Help Out

Your child may experience a lot of frustration when they aren't able to complete tasks or do something for themselves. One way of working around this is by allowing them to do things for other people. This can give them a real purpose in their life and something to look forward to, making the things they can't do seem less important.

Consider your child's interests and see if there is a charity organization where your child might be allowed to volunteer. If they aren't capable of doing physical volunteer work, consider giving a donation, such as food for an animal shelter, and taking your child with you to do the handover.

Mindful Coloring

Children with ASD often don't like to do any coloring due to them lacking the fine motor skills to color between the lines. Depending on your child's sensory preferences, the sound of the crayon on the paper may actually be very soothing for them. One way to make coloring more fun for them is by doing mindful coloring.

The purpose of this type of coloring isn't about making a pretty picture or staying between the lines. It's all about your child using their senses while they're coloring. This can be the feeling of the crayon in their hands, the smell of the crayon, the different bright colors, how it sounds when they move the crayon on the paper as they color, and so forth.

This can be a fantastic way for nonverbal children or those with severe ASD to get sensory stimulation and practice their fine motor skills.

While your child will have to do many of these exercises by themselves, it's important that you work on your little one's social skills and ability to build and maintain relationships with others. In the next chapter, we will explore this more, including tips on how to help your child communicate and manage their emotions more effectively.

5

TEACHING SOCIAL, EMOTIONAL, AND COMMUNICATION SKILLS

To help your child thrive in life, it's important to help them develop their social, emotional, communication, and problem-solving skills. These are three areas where children with ASD often struggle to cope and where their symptoms can make them stand out more. Think back to the societal stereotypes that we've discussed in Chapter 1. They all have to do with these three areas.

While the practical DBT exercises discussed in the previous chapters can go a long way in reducing the symptoms that can cause problems in these areas of the child's life, there are more specific exercises you can do to help your child develop these skills.

FIVE IMPORTANT SOCIAL SKILLS FOR CHILDREN WITH AUTISM

Social skills are vitally important for people to gain relationships with others, develop interests, and learn from others. Having good skills will result in your child being accepted by others more easily and giving them a sense of belonging. As a result, your child's mental health and quality of life will likely improve.

When it comes to developing social skills, there are generally four areas to focus on:

- **General or play skills**, such as sharing toys and taking turns.
- **Conversation skills**, including knowing what to say, what not to say, and what body language to use.
- **Emotional skills**, i.e., gaining empathy and understanding their own emotions.
- **Problem-solving skills** so that they can deal with conflict and make decisions.

All four of these areas can be extremely difficult for a child with ASD. When you're teaching your child these skills, remember to always include visual support. These can include pictures, words, prompt cards, or checklists, depending on your child's level of ASD and needs. For example, if you want your child to ask their aunt about their new baby, you can show them a picture of a baby. Or when you want your child to remember basic manners, you can give them prompt cards with the words "please" and "thank you" written on them. Adjust these according to your child's needs.

Let's look at five exercises that I've found to be effective in teaching a child with ASD much-needed social skills.

Become Actors

All children learn social skills through imitation, but because children with ASD often lack empathy, they may struggle a bit more to understand why certain things are acceptable and others are not. Since most children with ASD are visual learners, it can be helpful to act out certain scenarios with them rather than just letting them observe them. By doing this, you can explain what is happening and what the other person is likely feeling at every step of the way.

Be imaginative with this acting, but stick to routines or scenarios that your child might be familiar with. This way, your child can concentrate only on the social interaction without needing to learn about new situations they may not understand. You can even use a recent event in your child's life to act out. Let's say, for example, that your child recently fell and broke their arm. Now, you can pretend that their teddy bear took a fall and must go to the doctor.

Let your child pretend to be the doctor so that they can gain an understanding of how the other person in this familiar scenario experienced it:

- Help them to listen to the teddy bear's heartbeat.
- Let them do a quick physical exam to feel the teddy bear's body for any bumps.
- Put a bandage on the teddy's broken arm.
- Give the teddy bear a hug, sing them a song, or rock the bear back and forth—whatever your child usually prefers to feel better.

Next time you play this game, create a different scenario with a different toy. The more you do this, the more your child will begin to understand social skills and why things happen in certain ways. Over time, you can start to let them pretend the toy or teddy bear is their friend, or you can also take on the role of the friend. Guide your child gently by explaining to them if they're doing anything inappropriate.

Take Turns

All children struggle at times with waiting for their turns, but this can be an even more difficult task for children with ASD, who may struggle to understand why they need to wait and allow another friend to also have a chance. Many children with ASD also prefer to play by themselves, making this task even more difficult to understand.

Even if your child is happy to play by themselves, you need to teach them how to take part in activities where they'll have to share. Make this a fun activity by doing something your child enjoys. This way, your child will feel comfortable with the activity and only have to focus on the act of taking turns. For example, if they enjoy stacking all their blocks in a line, use this as a sharing activity. Divide the blocks between you and your child. Allow them to put down the first block and say, "Your turn." Once their block has been put down, say, "My turn," as you put a block down. Then say, "Your turn," as your child puts another block down. In between the turns, say something like, "It's fun to share" or "I love playing with you."

Your child might get upset when it's your turn. Try to stay calm and explain that you're playing together and that the same way they had a turn, you also get turns. They won't learn to participate in sharing activities on the first try. Just keep at it until they are able to do this.

Bring Out the Board Games

Board games can be a great way to teach your child social skills. Children with ASD generally enjoy these types of games, as there are strict rules that have to be followed. Depending on your child's capabilities, choose a game that they'll be able to enjoy. Take your time in reading the instructions and rules to them and make sure you follow these rules precisely. This will teach your child that they can have fun with another person and that there are rules that will make them feel safe.

Look at Others

Children often struggle with social situations, particularly when these situations are unfamiliar to them, out of fear of not understanding typical social cues. To make this even more difficult for them, many children tend to either overreact or underreact when they're put in certain situations. Since their reactions can be so different from those of their neurotypical peers, they can really struggle to understand the emotions of others and how to behave in a socially acceptable manner.

One way of doing this is by observing others with your child. There are various videos available online that show specific social situations and the emotions of people in these situations. Get your child's favorite snack and watch a video with them. Ask them what emotions they believe the people are showing and why. If your child isn't verbal, have the visual prompts ready for them to use. Explain to them why the people are having certain emotions and how the people in these videos are behaving as a result of these emotions. You can also ask them how they would feel if they were in a similar situation and how they would behave as a result of their emotions.

Do the Hula

Many children with ASD struggle to understand the personal space of others. This is largely due to sensory issues, which can result in them either standing too close to others or bumping into people by accident. The flip side of this can also be true: They may have an issue with others coming too close to them and touching them.

To help your child understand personal space, get two Hula-Hoops and have fun with your child:

- Put the Hula-Hoops on the ground next to each other.
- Stand in one of these hoops and ask your child to stand in the other hoop. Ask them how they feel with the distance between you, and explain

to them that this is a good distance to stand from others.

- Now, invite them into your space. You can say something like, "Do you want a hug?" or "Let's do a high five."
- Once the hug or high five is done, tell them to immediately return to their hoop. Explain to them that the only time you get closer to someone than the parameters of the hula is when that person invites you in, but that once this is done, they should always go back to their space.

WORKING ON YOUR CHILD'S COMMUNICATION SKILLS

Communication is another challenging area that many children with ASD struggle with. In general, there are three different types of communicators:

- Language, although it can be different from that of their neurotypical peers:
- They may repeat words heard on the TV in the wrong context or in a strange tone of voice.
- They may repeat the same words over and over.

- They may use the wrong pronouns; for example, "you" when referring to themselves and "I" when referring to someone else.
- Nonverbal communication:
- They might physically take someone to what they want.
- They might point at something and then look at you until you give them the desired object.
- They may use objects, such as pictures or prompt cards, to let the person know what they want.
- Communicating only through their behavior:
- They may throw tantrums, be aggressive towards others, or even harm themselves when they are upset, confused, or frightened.

When you work at improving a child with ASD's communication skills, it's important to do so gradually and explain words directly. Many with ASD don't understand sarcasm, so you'll only confuse your child if you don't talk to and teach them directly.

Watch your child while they're trying to communicate with you and help them with only the next step. Determine what method of communication they're using, as this will help you understand what next step you should guide them to.

When they're crying in the kitchen, your first instincts will likely be to teach them the words "food" or "hungry." However, those words aren't the logical next step in their communication skills. Since crying in the kitchen is behavioral communication, the next step would be nonverbal communication. Help them point at the food they want. Once they're able to communicate in a nonverbal manner, you can start to introduce the words "food" or "hungry."

Always remember to praise your child whenever they are learning a new skill. Just because they communicate only in a behavioral way, doesn't mean they can't understand what you're saying and when you're praising them. Show them that you notice what a big effort they're making.

Moving From Nonverbal to Verbal

If your child is currently a nonverbal communicator, there are various ways in which you can help your child learn more words. The next step for them would be to learn single words. Don't try to force sentences or big words on them. Just like a baby learns by saying single words, your child will learn in the same way.

Let's look at some tips on how you can get this done:

- Use very short sentences when you give them an instruction; for example, "Pants on," or "Kick ball." Once they start saying some of these words, you can include them in slightly longer sentences and gradually increase the length of the sentences you use.
- Use extremely simple language; for example, "Mud is yucky," or "Water is hot." Again, as their use of language improves, you can use more mature language.
- Exaggerate the tone of your voice to keep them interested in what you're saying and get the message across; for example, "The oven is 'very' hot, ouch."
- Ask your child questions that would need a reply; for example, "What color is this flower?" or "Are you hungry?" Start with questions that only need a single word as a response. You can gradually increase the length of the answer you need as their verbal skills develop. If your child simply nods instead of saying "yes," you can model what their answer should've been by saying "yes" while you nod the same way they did.

- Always make sure you give your child enough time to answer your questions. Their language skills are still developing, so they might need some time to understand your question and think about how they should answer it.
- If your child seems reluctant to talk, discuss topics that your child is really interested in. This might spur them to say a word or two.

As I've said before, always praise your child for any attempts they're making to communicate verbally. Remember, this is a massive milestone for them and should be celebrated.

Visual Cues

Throughout this book, we've discussed the value that written cues, schedules, or prompt cards can have for your child. Depending on your child's abilities, this doesn't have to just include pictures. It can also include words.

There is a big difference between being able to say words and reading them. It often happens that nonverbal children with ASD can read. If your child can learn to read, it's important to develop this skill as much as possible by adding words to their schedule or using visual reminders. This will help them to internalize language, which can eventually boost their chances of becoming more verbal. Always remember to use words on these visual reminders that your child can easily understand, and gradually increase the difficulty of these words. Whenever you add a new word, make sure you explain it to them to make sure they understand it.

Gestures

If your child is nonverbal, they might use gestures to communicate what they want and need. These gestures might not always be as simple as pointing to something. They may develop their own gestures. It's important that you try your best to learn these gestures. When your child is using a specific gesture, repeat this gesture while saying the appropriate word. Over time, your child may learn to associate certain gestures with words and develop their language skills accordingly. You can also create visual cards that you can show them for each gesture to develop their communication skills even more.

Use the Quiet Times

As much as it's important to talk to your child to develop their language skills, you should make sure you allow your child enough quiet time to process their thoughts and the words they're hearing. They might also need time to think about ways to respond, so if you're constantly talking to them, they may not have the quiet space to try to talk. Find the middle ground between teaching your child better language skills and giving them a chance to communicate.

Do It Together

Sometimes the best thing you can do for your child is to simply spend time with them. This way you can bond with your little one, help increase trust in your relationship, and develop their skills.

Drawing with your child can be a great way of doing this. You don't need to be an artist to do this; your child won't care what your picture looks like. All that's important is that you spend time together doing something they enjoy.

Use drawing time to help them make associations. If your child draws something, then draw something next to it that goes with it; for example, if your child draws a ball, you can draw a bat next to it. If your child draws an apple, you can draw a banana.

You can also use these drawing times to help your child develop social skills. A fun way of doing this is to create your own comic strips. Create characters that your child can identify with. Every time you have drawing time, add another strip to your comic. Add scenarios in these comic strips that will make it fun and provide a lesson for your child.

Playing music is another great activity you can do with your child. You can use drums, shakers, or any other instrument that your child might enjoy. Keep the noise level to what your child is comfortable with on that day. Let your child create the beat and follow along with them. Dance with your child while you play music and let your bodies do the communicating.

HOW TO TEACH YOUR CHILD EMOTIONAL REGULATION

Emotional regulation is about managing your emotions and changing your behaviors accordingly. This skill is very important when you experience difficult emotions, such as anger, frustration, and anxiety. These are emotions that many children with ASD have to deal with on a daily basis. When they aren't able to control their emotions and adapt their behaviors accordingly, they may react in ways that may appear to be over-the-top, socially inappropriate, and at times even aggressive. This can not only help them cope better in social situations but also help them cope better with life in general.

To help your child manage their emotions more successfully, you first need to make sure your child understands at least the most basic emotions and can identify these emotions within themselves. Start out with the most basic emotions, such as happy, sad, and angry. As your child learns to understand these emotions, you can gradually add more complex ones.

Explain to your child how they typically react when they have these emotions. You can do this by either discussing it with them, creating a story about it, or even singing them a song. Do whatever your child prefers. When you want to improve your child's behavior, focus on good reactions to certain emotions rather than constantly telling them their behavior is wrong.

There are various ways in which you can help your child with this. Let's look at some exercises that have proven to be very effective in helping children with ASD understand and manage their emotions more successfully.

Name the Emotions

One of the easiest ways to teach a child about emotions is by labeling them every time they feel them. Doing this provides a few benefits:

- Your child will learn the name of the emotion.

- Your child will understand how this emotion feels.
- Your child will realize that what they're feeling is simply an emotion they can control.
- Your child will realize that they can choose to react in a way that may go against the emotion they're feeling.

Start by first just naming the emotion; for example, "You're sad," or "I can see you're happy." If your child's ASD is very severe, you may choose to only use the name of the emotion; for example, "Sad" or "Happy." If your child's ASD is very mild, you can take this a step further by saying something like, "I can see you're very sad about this. It's okay to feel this way, but it's not okay to react in this way." Always help them to understand when their behavior isn't ideal and what a better way would be for them to deal with these emotions.

If your child is able to, let them say the name of the emotion with you. Eventually, they'll be able to identify these emotions by themselves. When your child hears the emotion being expressed out loud, their brain will be able to process it more easily. This will also force your child to pause, and in the time that they take to say the name of this emotion, they will have time to cool off.

Create an Emotions Chart

If your child is nonverbal and can't say the name of their emotions, you can create a visual emotion chart that helps them better understand their emotions. Start out with the basic emotions that your child can understand well and feel often. Print pictures that depict these emotions. Many people use emojis for this. Next, create a calendar for each day of the month.

Add "emotion time" into your child's schedule and make it part of their routine to think about emotions. Choose a time of day when your child must choose a picture portraying the emotions that they're experiencing. Help them to paste this on the calendar for that day. This will help them understand what they're feeling, and you'll also be able to see easily if there's a pattern in their behavior or if there's an imbalance in their emotions. For example, if your child constantly chooses sad pictures, it can be an indication that they're depressed and might need more help.

If you don't want to create a calendar, you can let them crumple up the picture of the emotion they're feeling and throw it away. You can even create baskets for different emotions by adding rocks. Let them take a rock out of the emotion basket they're feeling and throw it into a bush. Doing this will teach your child that they have power over their emotions and can choose to get over them without reacting to them.

Chartes for Good and Bad Behaviors

Another visual chart that may be very beneficial for your child is one that depicts good and bad behaviors. Create a chart with the emotions they understand, with spaces where you can list good behaviors associated with this emotion as well as bad ones. This way, your child can look at the chart when they're feeling certain emotions and be reminded of better ways to behave.

Help Them With Coping Strategies

While charts for good and bad behaviors can be helpful to teach your child about appropriate behaviors, you can take this a step further by teaching them different coping strategies. One way of doing this is by creating hypothetical situations during playtime and role-playing how they would react and how you would behave in the same situation. Then you can talk about what kind of behavior each of you chose, which ones would be the most effective and appropriate, and why.

You can also create scenario cards for your child. These cards can be helpful in teaching your child to recognize emotions, what the outcome of different behaviors according to these emotions would be, and how you can react positively to each one. Add different scenarios to different cards. Explain the situation to them. Ask them how the people in the scenario must be feeling and what your child believes the best reaction would be.

Once your child can identify emotions effectively and determine what the best behavior would be, you can teach them some coping strategies. Depending on your child's abilities, the following can be techniques you can teach them:

- **Take deep breaths**: Breathing techniques are a wonderful and easy way to help your child calm down when their emotions are getting the better of them. Refer back to Chapter 4 and the breathing techniques discussed there, such as *Square Breathing, Hot Chocolate Breath,* and *Balloon Breath.*
- **Count to 20**: Let your child count to 20 to calm down. If your child is unable to count, you can create counting baskets for them. To do this, you need two baskets and 20 things they can use to transfer from one basket to the other to create the illusion of counting. Many people use little balls for this. Once your child has moved all 20 balls from one basket to the next, they would've had time to calm down.

- **Ask for help**: Always remind your child that it's okay to ask for help when they're struggling. If they are nonverbal, they can use their gestures or visual cards to ask for help.
- **Think of a compromise**: If your child has a milder form of ASD, help them to think of ways they might be able to compromise to reduce any conflict they might experience and cope with their difficult situations more effectively. Remind your child that they are allowed to have their own boundaries in place, but that there might be times when they'll have to adjust these boundaries slightly to maintain and build their relationships with others.
- **Walk away**: In many situations, the best way to cope with a difficult situation will be to simply walk away. Talk to your child about what their "hard-no" is, and help them identify situations where it will be better for them to walk away from a situation. Learning how to do this can help save your child a lot of heartache and unhappiness.

Create a Calm Down Caddy

Give your child a sense of safety by creating a calm down caddy for them. This will be a box or basket containing all the things they may need to calm themselves down and can include noise-canceling headphones, stress balls, something to bite, or a fidget toy. Think about your child's preferences and what usually helps them stay calm in difficult situations.

I would suggest making a few calming caddies for your child to make it easily accessible for them. Also, make one that they can take with them when they leave the house.

Create Emotions Zones

Another way you can teach your child to regulate their emotions and adjust their behavior accordingly is by creating different zones in which they can group their feelings. This can be a great tool to improve your child's self-control, let them become more aware of what they're feeling, and build emotional resilience. By using different emotion zones, your child will become more aware of what they're feeling, and then their behavior will become less regulated.

To do this, create three emotion zones. I prefer using traffic light colors to do this, as this way they will learn to understand these road markings as well:

- **Red zone**: This is the zone for extreme and intense emotions. They include anger, rage, terror, sadness, and even excessive elation.

When your child is experiencing "red zone" emotions, they may struggle to cope with what's going on in their life and behave in over-the-top and aggressive ways.

- **Yellow zone**: This is the zone for emotions that are heightened but not at a dangerous level yet. They can include stress, worry, restlessness, and excitement. When your child has emotions in the "yellow zone," they should be careful that they manage these emotions as quickly as possible before they go over to the "red zone."
- **Green zone**: This is the zone for calmness and contentment. When your child experiences "green zone" emotions, which can also include happiness and eagerness to learn, their behavior will likely be under control.

Once your child understands the different zones their emotions fall under, you can create zones in your home; for example, the quietest area of your home can become their "red zone," a place with things that can distract them from their emotions can be their "yellow zone," and the rest of the home can be their "green zone." When your child realizes they're experiencing emotions outside of the "green zone," they should immediately go to the zone identified for those emotions. They can then stay there to cool-off and go back to their "green zone" emotions.

If your child spends a lot of time outside your home, you can get specific objects that they can identify with the red and yellow zones; for example, a red stress ball for the "red zone" and a yellow fidget toy for the "yellow zone." Make sure you always have these with you. When your child reaches for one of these toys, you'll know that they're experiencing difficult feelings and that they might need your help to cope.

Co-Regulation With Your Child

There will likely be times when you and your child will experience similar emotions at the same time. When this happens, it can be very helpful if you work with your child to manage them. This will help your child realize that they're not the only ones experiencing these negative emotions, and you can model better ways of dealing with them.

If you and your child are both feeling sad, you can tell them something like, "It looks like you're very sad. I'm also sad. Why don't we try to help each other feel happy again?" By saying something like this, you've identified the emotion that you're both feeling, and your child will understand that you're feeling the same as them and that you will work together to feel positive again. A quick fix to help them overcome extreme negative emotions is to watch silly videos with them. There are many of these videos available online. Laugh with your child. After a while, ask them something like, "I'm feeling better now. Are you also feeling a bit less sad?" If they agree, praise them by telling them you've done magic together by getting rid of the sadness.

DEVELOPING YOUR CHILD'S PROBLEM-SOLVING SKILLS

Teaching your child problem-solving skills will help them not only cope with difficult social situations more effectively but also boost their independence. This can be a difficult task for children with ASD to learn due to language and communication barriers they may face, as well as being over-stimulated quicker than their neurotypical peers.

One way of doing this is to give your child instructions that incorporate specific activities. In the beginning, your child might struggle to carry out these instructions, so help them with any steps they may have difficulty with:

- Use visual aids whenever you can, especially when you're just starting to teach them these problem-solving skills.

- Repeat the instructions as many times as you have to.
- Break down the instruction into quick, doable tasks.
- Praise them for every step they're able to do.

Always remember that the more you help them practice solving problems, the quicker they will grasp the concept and be able to solve problems independently.

Picture Problems

Use different pictures that depict some sort of problem to help your child reason and solve problems. This is especially helpful if your child is a visual learner. It's always best if you can use pictures of things or places that your child is familiar with. If you can't create your own pictures, there are various pictures available online that you can use to help your child learn these skills:

- Show your child the picture.
- Ask them what the problem in the picture is.
- Next, let them come up with different ways in which they think the problem could be solved.
- Discuss all of their suggestions, no matter how ridiculous they may seem. Look at the pros and

cons of each and help them understand why this won't solve the problem.

- If none of their suggestions are helpful, make your own suggestions on how this problem can be solved.

If your child is nonverbal but can draw, they can try to draw their solution to the problem or use their gestures or visual aids to try and explain these solutions to you.

Organize the Steps

Another visual activity you can do to help your child solve problems is to have different cards depicting the problem and the solution. Let's look at an example of a ball falling on the roof of a house. If your child enjoys playing with a ball, this can be something they might be familiar with:

- The first picture can be of a child playing with a ball.
- The second picture is of the ball lying on the roof of the house.
- Then, have about three different pictures showing different ways of solving the problem. This can include trying to climb the wall, using a ladder, or using a tool such as a broom to try to get the ball down.

- Let your child look through the solutions and choose the one they believe would be best. Ask them to explain why they decided on that solution and why they think it's better than the other possible solutions.
- Have another card ready for each of those solutions; for example, the child falling while trying to climb the wall to show that solution is not good, the broom getting stuck in the gutter of the house, and the child safely getting the ball down by using a ladder.
- Finish with the last card showing the child playing with the ball again.
- Once your child has worked through the different cards, give them all the cards and let them sequence the cards in the right order. Do note that children with neurodiversity may struggle with organizing steps like this. If they struggle, do it with them and explain why every card should come next.

Get Some Power

Children with a milder form of ASD can also benefit from the acronym *POWER*. This is a relatively easy one to learn and will remind your child the whole time that they have the power to make their own decisions and can solve their problems.

The steps for this exercise are as follows:

- **Put your problem into words or visuals**: Help your child to identify the problem they're facing and put this problem into their own words. If they struggle with this, teach them to fill in the blanks in this sentence: I was _____ and then _____. This will make it easier for them to understand exactly what they were doing before they encountered the problem and what the problem is. If they're nonverbal, they can use their visual aids to do all these steps.

- **Observe your emotions**: Ask them to describe the emotions they felt when they realized what their problem was. Ask them to explain why they felt these emotions and how intense they were. If they're able to, ask them to rate the intensity of these emotions from one to ten. Otherwise, let them use their emotion zones to describe how extreme their emotions were.

- **Work out what you want to achieve**: Ask them what outcome they would like to achieve in solving this problem. Explain to them that by understanding what they would like to see happen, they will be able to think of possible solutions to their problems a lot easier. Make sure that their goals are realistic and achievable.

- **Explore all the possible solutions**: Encourage your child to think of different solutions that would bring them closer to achieving their goal. Explore each of their suggestions. Talk about why it can work and what may make it difficult for this solution to pan out. If they can't come up with a solution by themselves, help them find one by making suggestions. Always make sure their chosen solution is fair, safe, effective, and possible. Do some role-playing where your child can practice implementing their solution.

- **Review your plan**: After the solution has been implemented, talk about whether it worked and what might be better in the future. If your child was able to solve the problem, praise them by saying something like, "You should really be proud of yourself." If the solution didn't solve their problem, repeat the previous steps to come up with a better solution to try.

While you're helping your child learn all these skills, it's absolutely vital that you do this with acceptance and by showing compassion toward your child. In the next chapter, we'll look at ways you can do this.

6

ACCEPTING YOUR CHILD WITH COMPASSION

While parenting a child with ASD, there will likely be many times when you get frustrated with your child and their symptoms. It can feel like nothing you're doing is helping or making life easier. You might even start to question your role as a parent and why you were blessed with a child with such unique needs.

Whenever you feel defeated and frustrated, remember that what your child is going through is likely much worse. Their situation can be difficult enough without having parents who judge them. They need parents who accept them with compassion and show them love, no matter how dire the situation may seem.

The first step in doing this is by becoming an expert on your child, their triggers, how different things affect them, and how you can prevent certain explosive behaviors. Then you should accept your child, difficulties and all. Focus on the positives, try to enjoy any quirks your child may have, celebrate any successes you may achieve, no matter how small they might be, and most of all, love your child no matter what.

Doing this will not only help you gain confidence in your parenting abilities, it can also help your child tremendously. Never give up. Instead, be there for your child every step of the way.

BE YOUR CHILD'S CHEERLEADER

All parents have many different roles to fill and often have more responsibilities than they ever thought were possible. When your child has ASD, these responsibilities can seem never-ending. One of the most important responsibilities you may have is to be your child's cheerleader.

Your support can change the course of their lives and help them thrive and gain independence. Let's look at the different ways you can do this.

Your Child Didn't Choose Their Condition

The same way you didn't choose to have a child with ASD, they didn't choose to have the condition either. They can't help having their symptoms. They didn't choose to constantly feel panicked, confused, and overwhelmed. They didn't choose to live in a world that they don't understand and where most people make no effort to understand them. If they could choose, they would opt to be neurotypical.

That being said, your child is more than just their diagnosis. Their ASD doesn't define who they are. It's simply a part of who they are as a person.

Your Child Loves You

Many children with severe ASD will struggle with showing affection. If you're a parent of one of these children, this lack of affection can make it feel like your efforts and hard work aren't appreciated or even recognized. All you may want is for your child to hug you and tell you that they love you.

Always remember that love means different things to different people, and not everyone will show it in the same way. Your child might show that they love you when you're the only one that can calm them down or when they insist on lying on top of you at night. They may show you love when they do what you're asking them to do, no matter how difficult it may be for them. They may even show you love by asking you to do things for them.

Ultimately, you're probably the most important person in their lives. They do love you, even if they don't show it in typical ways. Remember this when times are tough, and continue to show them love in your way.

All Parents Have Struggles

Everyone is different, and so are their struggles. No matter how some parents may want to show off their picture-perfect children and their achievements on social media, remember that they also have struggles. Your child's challenges may just be more obvious than those of these people and their children. But, trust me, on some level, everyone struggles.

See the World Through Their Eyes

Whenever you get upset, irritated, or frustrated by your child's explosive behaviors, try to view the situation from their perspective. Ask yourself what happened to make them so upset and what you can do to try to help them overcome this. Continue to help them manage their emotions. Do the exercises to improve your child's distress tolerance.

Don't Take Their Outbursts Personally

You might get badly upset by your child's behavior. Always remember, it's not a reflection on you as their parent. Be as patient as you possibly can with your child. Try to understand why they are behaving in certain ways, and try to mitigate the situations. However, sometimes there may be times when you'll have to let them cry or scream. This is not a reflection on you or your parenting abilities. Your child might just have a difficult day. Accept this and treat them with compassion.

Talk and Teach Tolerance

A big source of challenges that many children with ASD must face on a daily basis, is lack of understanding and tolerance from other people. Help your child by advocating their condition and explaining to as many people as you can about ASD. The more you open up about your child's conditions and explain to others what they're actually about, the more you can reduce the societal stereotypes in your child's immediate circle. Show them that your child is more than just a condition by treating them with love, respect, and tolerance.

Ask for Help

There will likely be days when you just can't continue. Don't be too hard on yourself when this happens.

Instead, seek out help. If you have a loved one that your child is comfortable with, ask them to babysit, if only for 15 minutes, so that you can have a break. Speak to your child's teacher. They might have suggestions for new things you can try with your child. Find out about support groups in your area. That way, you can get to know other parents of children with ASD and share your experiences in a safe environment.

SHOW YOUR CHILD LOVE

Showing love to others doesn't just mean telling the person you love them and giving them a hug. There are many other ways you can show love. The more love you show your child, the more likely it is for them to thrive, feel safe, and learn new skills. Let's look at some less obvious ways you can show your child that you love them.

Support Them and Their Interests

People with ASD often have very specific and intense interests. Observe your child closely to identify some of their interests. Pick one or two of their interests to focus on, and go out of your way to show your child that you share these interests. This can mean getting them equipment to practice this interest, finding others with the same interests that they can have discussions with, or simply learning more about it so that you can show your child that you care about them and the things that are important to them.

Give Them Structure

In general, children with ASD thrive when they have strict routines and structures in their lives. One of the best things you can do for your child is adhere to a routine that meets their needs. This will give them the sense of safety they desperately need and make them feel loved and accepted.

Ask Their Opinion

Never assume that you know what your child will want. Treat them with the respect that you'd want to be treated with by asking them their opinions on things. This will not only make them feel seen and heard, but you will also gain a lot of insight into what makes your child tick. This can greatly reduce the level of frustration you and your child may experience, as you'll know exactly what they want and need and will be able to give it to them in a way they prefer.

Assume the Best

A lot of people assume that just because someone has ASD, they aren't capable of doing things. This couldn't be further from the truth. People with ASD can achieve greatness. Always assume that your child will be able to achieve things. Remember, greatness doesn't have to mean making a scientific discovery. Greatness can also mean being able to cope with their condition and lead a relatively independent life. Show your child you believe in them.

Let Go of Your Expectations

Many people go into parenthood with unrealistic expectations of having perfect children who will listen to them, obey rules, and achieve perfect grades. Hanging on to these expectations is a sure way of being disappointed and feeling frustrated with your situation. Instead, accept your reality. You have a beautiful child that needs you. Focus on your child, not on their condition or the expectations of parenthood you might've had.

Embrace Their Way of Coping

Your child's way of coping with challenges in life might include stimming. Never try to stop their stims. They're trying to come to terms with what they're going through. They're trying to soothe themselves in a world filled with things they don't understand and people who don't understand them. Instead, embrace your child's stimming instead of suppressing it. Tell your child that you're proud of them for knowing what they can do to make life easier for themselves. If they'll allow you to, join them in their stimming. This can be a great bonding moment for the two of you.

Educate Them on Their Condition

Teaching your child about their condition can make life a lot less scary. They will understand why they are different from most other people in their lives and that this is okay. They will understand why they can't understand so many things, and this may give them the peace of mind to accept this instead of fighting against it. When you're explaining your child's condition to them, do this in the most positive way possible and constantly reassure them that this is nothing to fear or feel ashamed of. It's simply something that is a small part of the amazing person they are.

FOSTERING HEALTHY RELATIONSHIPS AMONG OTHER FAMILY MEMBERS

Raising your child with ASD can be a consuming task, which can easily result in neglecting your relationships with other family members, however unintentional it may be. To help your child thrive in life, it's important to constantly work on having positive family relationships.

Being surrounded by positive and loving relationships will help your child feel secure and will improve their confidence and willingness to learn new skills. It will give them a healthy example of the type of relationships they should strive for, and it will make it easier for them to solve problems and respect others.

Working on the relationships within your family can be done by focusing on three aspects:

- Working on the relationships between all members of the family.
- Focusing on the strengths of your family.
- Improving your family's resilience.

Let's start out by focusing on your relationship with your partner. If you're a single parent, you can skip over this one and focus on your relationships with your other children. If you only have one child, you can skip over the relationships you have with other family members.

Your Relationship With Your Partner

Raising a child with special needs can bring couples closer together, as they can learn love, respect, compassion, and patience through seeing how they help and care for their child together.

It can, however, have the opposite effect, as caring for a child with ASD can bring big challenges and put additional stress on a family. For example, a child with ASD will likely need some sort of support, be it in the form of therapy or other medical visits. The bill for these treatments can easily climb, causing financial strain. Due to the needs of your child, one parent might have to stay at home to be the child's full-time carer. This can also put strain on the relationship. These stressors can result in one partner resenting the other, particularly if the caring duties aren't shared fairly, or even blaming each other for your child's condition.

If this is the case for you and your partner, it's important to spend as much time as your schedule allows together. Try to have fun, no matter how difficult life may get at times. Talk to each other about your frustrations and fears. Listen when the other person talks, so you can understand their point of view. Discuss the workload of caring for your child and where adjustments can be made to spread the responsibilities more fairly. Never be afraid to seek help. No matter how high your medical bills might be, if you and your partner need counseling to overcome the challenges in your lives, it will be worth it.

Relationships With Your Other Children

If you have more than one child, it is important to make a conscious effort to get your children to bond with each other. Your neurotypical children might resent your child with ASD, as they might feel like this child is getting all the attention. This is why it's so important to spend time with your other children.

If your schedule allows it, spend time alone with each of your children as frequently as is possible. Make sure that, even though you might give your other child more attention, they're loved and important. The stronger your relationship is with your other children, the easier it will be for them to accept their sibling with ASD.

Apart from spending time alone with your children, make sure all your children do things together. Let them do an activity that they are all capable of and can enjoy together. Let them laugh together.

Your Relationship With Other Family Members

Having strong relationships with other family members can give your children a sense of belonging and provide you the support system you'll need during the challenging times. Include your children's grandparents, aunts, uncles, cousins, and friends in your lives as much as possible.

Make sure they have all the information they may need to understand your child's conditions, their needs, and their typical behavior. Make sure they understand that your child's stimming is not something to frown upon or be afraid of, that it's simply a way for them to cope with life's stressors.

Invite your trusted family members over as much as possible so that they can get to know your children and build relationships with them. They might be able to fulfill needs in your other children's lives while you're busy caring for your child with ASD. Make an effort for them to spend time with your child with ASD to build a trusting relationship.

Focusing on Your Family's Strengths

While you're working on improving the relationships with your different family members, take note of the different strengths that these relationships offer. By focusing on the strengths of each family member and the different relationships, you'll be able to use these to build even stronger connections within your family. Let's look at some ways in which you can do this:

- Consider the different things your family enjoys doing and find activities that everyone in the family can enjoy. Write them down while you think of them. Think of activities that take different lengths of time to complete—your family's schedule won't allow you to spend hours together doing something. When you think about these types of activities, you might even come up with something that will take less than 30 minutes to complete. Look at your list often, and try your best to do at least one of these activities every week.

- Build practicing gratitude into your family routines; for example, every night when you sit down for dinner, let every family member name one thing that they're grateful for that day. In the beginning, some of your children might say something like, "I'm grateful for water," or "I'm grateful for food." That is fine. It's something that they're happy to have. Over time, you can encourage them to think a bit deeper. Eventually, they might say something like, "I'm grateful for every member of my family." This activity can help bring the family closer together by focusing on what you're all grateful for having.

- Another family activity you can do together is to give each family member a pen and paper and ask them to write down one positive aspect about each family member. Try to do this at least once a week, and give every family member a chance to share their list with others. This will be a fantastic bonding opportunity, as you'll essentially be praising each other the whole time.

- Once you have a list of the strengths from doing the exercise above, make time to discuss at least one strength from each family member together. Ask your family for ideas on how you can use this strength to either do an activity together or include it in your daily routine to make life easier for everyone.

Building Your Family's Resilience

Resilience is a person's ability to get back up again after going through difficult times. The more resilience your family has together, the stronger the relationships will get. Let's look at ways in which you can build your family's resilience:

- Make sure all members of your family understand ASD and can talk about it with others. This will not only help them understand your child with ASD, but you will also put them in a position where they can show their commitment to their family by explaining something about ASD to someone else. Make sure they understand that ASD is not something to be ashamed of and that they're allowed to talk about it with their friends.

- Make a big deal of the contributions your child with ASD makes to the household, even if it's just something small like making sure everyone sticks to the routine. This will help to make this child feel like they belong and let your other children understand that, even though this child may get more attention, they also play their part.

- Always encourage all members of your family to play a role in the distribution of roles and responsibilities in the house. Assign everyone a chore, and make sure they understand that you're all working together as a team.

- Always work on solving problems together as a family. Talk about things that might cause conflict, listen to everyone's point of view, and find solutions that are fair to everyone.

- Be as positive as you can, no matter how difficult your circumstances may be. Teach your children to look for the silver lining in all situations.

Having strong relationships within your family can help to make the extremely rough days that may come with your child's ASD easier to deal with. In the next chapter, we'll look at ways you can manage your own emotions more successfully to reduce stress.

7

STAYING STRONG ON
ROUGH DAYS

P arenting a child with ASD can be stressful and filled with many rough days. Your emotions may feel like you're on a rollercoaster, going from extreme highs filled with excitement and elation when your child learns a new skill to the lowest of lows filled with feelings of frustration, overwhelm, sadness, guilt, anger, confusion, and depression.

Frustration can set in quickly, not just due to your child's inability to do things, but also when others don't understand your child's condition and judge them unnecessarily. You might feel anxious, not just over what the day might hold but also for your child's future. You might feel guilty, blaming yourself for your child's condition, not doing things right, or getting angry with your child. You might feel angry over not having the help you might need in caring for your child or even with your child for behaving in the way they do.

All of these emotions, as normal as they are, can make it difficult to handle your stress effectively, which will only negatively impact your child and their ability to learn new skills. This is why it's so important to be able to manage your emotions effectively to have better control over your reactions.

Doing the exercises mentioned in Chapter 5 on how to teach your child emotional regulation can be just as beneficial for you as becoming more aware of what you're feeling, how you would usually behave, and deciding to behave in a better way. While you're practicing with your child, do it by yourself as well and see how you're both gaining power over your emotions.

HOW TO REDUCE STRESS AND MANAGE YOUR EMOTIONS

There are likely many specific situations in your daily life that may make it difficult for you to gain control over your emotions. My personal worst one was the meltdowns my child used to have in stores or other public spaces. Let's look at some aspects of your life that can make it more difficult to manage your stress and how you can overcome them.

Dealing With Meltdowns

How many times have you tried to stop a meltdown as quickly as possible? You hate having almost all the people in the entire store stare at you with judgment written all over their faces. You hate seeing your little one so upset and struggling to control what they're feeling. And you're tired, your patience is running low, and you just want to get what you need from the store and get home in peace and quiet.

Unfortunately, one trip to a single store can easily result in more than just one or two meltdowns. Sometimes, it can feel like the meltdown song is stuck on repeat and you're desperately trying to diffuse one situation after the other.

When you're going through this, remember that a child with ASD doesn't cry or stim with the purpose of getting at you. The causes of their meltdowns are, in most cases, completely different from those of neurotypical toddlers, who will throw themselves down over wanting a new toy.

Children with ASD have meltdowns because they can't cope with what's going on around them. They need to release the tension that's likely been building up since you left for the store. They might be overwhelmed by sensory stimulation, such as a tag on the shirt scratching their skin or someone talking too loudly in the next aisle.

The sooner I came to terms with the fact that my son's brain is wired differently and, as a result, will react to things in his life in his own way, the sooner I started to gain control over myself when I was in situations like these. I learned to put my own emotions aside and, in that moment of meltdown, focus only on what my son needed. This is what I found to be helpful:

- **Have empathy**: Listen to your child, acknowledge their feelings, and never judge them, regardless of how infuriating the situation may be. When you validate their feelings, they will feel heard. This will make such a big impact on your child who likely often feels misunderstood and not heard. Now is not the time to tell them to stop crying. Focus only on making sure your child feels understood.
- **Make sure they feel safe and loved**: No matter what you say to your child while they're having a meltdown, the chances are good that your child will be so overwhelmed that they won't hear a word. Instead of trying to explain to them why their behavior is wrong, just sit with them or stand close to them. Make sure they

feel loved and safe. Show them you're there for them by staying close to them.

- **Leave the punishments**: Punishments are meant to stop intentional misbehaving. When children with ASD have meltdowns, they can't control their emotions and behavior. Therefore, they shouldn't be punished for it. If you try to punish a child with ASD for having a meltdown, you'll likely just cause the child to feel shame, fear, and anxiety instead of helping them overcome their overwhelming emotions.

- **Forget the bystanders**: Ask parents what they find to be the worst part about public meltdowns, and many will say it's the judgmental looks from bystanders. I've found meltdowns became easier to manage the instant I stopped caring about people staring at my child and me. Next time your child is having a meltdown, make the mindset change by realizing that the opinions of onlookers don't matter. The only thing that matters at that point is helping your little one through this difficult experience. Allow the bystanders to look all they want while you focus only on your child.

- **Have a calm-down caddy ready**: Always make sure you have a small calm-down caddy with you when you go anywhere. However, when your child is having a meltdown, don't force any of the tools or toys in the caddy on them. Simply open the caddy and put it close to them. If you want, show them that their caddy is there, but don't force anything into your child's hands. Allow your child to cry for as long as they need to until they reach for something in their caddy.

- **Remind them of coping skills once the meltdown is over**: Once your child has calmed down, you can remind them of the coping skills you're trying to teach them. It can be best to only do this once your child has been removed from the environment where the meltdown took place and their emotions have returned to the "green zone."

Some of these may be small changes from how you used to handle your child's meltdowns. However, if you make sure you always treat your child with empathy, compassion, and love, you and your child will get there.

Make Time for Yourself

Your emotions will easily get the better of you if you don't have any time for yourself. If you continue doing this, you might find yourself on a slippery slope to burnout. Make it a priority to spend time by yourself, even if it's just 20 minutes or so. You need this downtime. If you have a partner, ask them to take care of your child during this time so that you can rest. If not, look at finding an activity that your child can do safely by themselves so that you can do something you enjoy or lie down for a few minutes. Don't bargain on doing this once your child is asleep at night. You'll likely be so tired that you won't enjoy this time by yourself.

Stop Asking, "What If?"

We've already discussed the importance of accepting your child's condition, but this is such a life changing aspect that I had to include it again here. Ask yourself, "How often do I wonder what my life could've been like if my child didn't have ASD?" If you're honest with yourself, you might be shocked at how often this happens.

Yes, it's only natural to wish you had a simpler life without the challenges your child's condition brings. This is probably even more the case when it comes to worrying about your child's future, whether they'll ever be able to live independently, and what will happen to them when you aren't there to care for them anymore.

Change your mindset from the "what ifs" to the "right now." This will help you become more mindful by focusing on what your child needs from you right now. Focus on the present instead of worrying about the future.

Turn Your Emotions Into Opposite Behaviors

Whenever life gets too much and your emotions overwhelm you, remind yourself that you're only human and will have emotions. Accept the fact that some of your emotions may be very negative at times, and that's okay. Instead of worrying about your emotions and feeling guilty over them, focus on reacting in the opposite way. If you're feeling sad, make an effort to force yourself to be happy. If you're frustrated and overwhelmed, do what you need to so that you can feel peaceful and content. Tell yourself, "I'm feeling frustrated with my situation, and that's okay. But, I choose to feel peaceful." By naming your negative emotion and how you'd like to feel, your brain will find a way to bring peace to your life.

Make Small Changes

Overcoming the stress that your child's ASD may bring isn't an easy task that will happen overnight. Instead, it will take a daily effort, taking it one step at a time. I would recommend that you start out by making small changes to how you handle your stress. Sometimes the smallest action can spur big results. It can be something like counting to ten every time you feel like your stress is getting the better of you or doing breathing techniques to calm yourself down. You might even decide that if you can't change your stress, you should make your body stronger by doing some exercises. There are many applications you can download onto your smartphone that will guide you through exercises you can easily do in the comfort of your living room.

Know When You Need Help

There's no shame in admitting that you need help. In fact, I find this ability to become vulnerable to be one of the strongest attributes a person can have. If you don't seek help when you need it, you will push yourself beyond the limit of what you can handle, which won't benefit you or your child. Whether this help is informal, such as asking a close friend or family member to help you out in some way, or more formal, such as getting a carer for your child (even if it's only for a day or two a week) or seeking out counseling, do what you need to. Remember, you can't pour from an empty cup. Make sure you fill your cup by taking care of yourself.

Practice Self-Care

One way to fill your cup is by making self-care a priority. You don't need to devote hours every day to doing this. Just make sure you make an effort to look after yourself. Not only will this benefit your physical health, but also your mental health. It will help you stay calm when you have rough days.

Let's look at some simple things you can do to take care of yourself:

- **Spend time in nature.** This can mean going for a walk in the park or working in the garden. There are many activities you can do in nature that your child will be able to participate in, so your child will also directly benefit from doing this.
- **Look at your diet and make sure you eat as healthy as possible.** Yes, when the stress of life gets to us, it's easy to reach for a home delivery takeout, but the amount of oil, salt, and preservatives in this food will only decrease your mental health even more. Instead, opt for as many fresh fruits and vegetables as you can.
- **Make sure you drink enough water.** The difference that a couple of glasses of water daily can make to how you feel physically and mentally is astounding. Make it interesting by slicing some lemon or cucumber into your water.
- **Create a healthy sleeping routine.** Aim for between six and eight hours of proper sleep

every night. If your child is a difficult sleeper, this might sound like an impossible task. However, instead of bingeing on a TV show before you fall asleep, read a page or two in a book to help your brain switch off and stay away from screens just before bedtime. Make the most of the precious time you have for sleeping.

JOURNAL YOUR CHILD'S DEVELOPMENT

While you're busy caring for your child day in and day out it's easy to lose sight of the progress they've made. Keeping a journal of your child's development is an easy way to keep you focused on what you need to do. Knowing how far you've already come in your child's development will motivate you to continue on the difficult days when you want to give up.

Keeping a journal on your child will also help you to pick up on any small signs that your child isn't well. This will be particularly handy if your child is nonverbal and can't tell you clearly when they aren't feeling well. You'll also get a clearer picture of the techniques that have helped your child cope.

I would recommend you include the following in your child's journal:

- foods and drinks consumed
- activities your child enjoyed
- favorite toy for the day
- activities your child didn't want to take part in
- your child's emotions and behaviors
- what helped calm them down
- any sensory sensitivities
- any illnesses or pains

While you'll keep a daily tab on the above, make sure to note in the journal when you start teaching them a new skill and when they are able to use this new skill for the first time. Noting the dates will help you understand how long your child actually needs to learn a skill, which will be very helpful for planning purposes going forward when you want to introduce another skill.

Throughout the previous few chapters, we've explored the value that being mindful in your parenting can bring. In the last chapter, we'll look at some specific techniques you can introduce to be more mindful.

8

PRACTICING MINDFULNESS
WITH YOUR CHILD

B eing mindful is an easy way to forget about the worries and fears you may have about your child's condition or future and help you focus on what you need to do that day. It also holds amazing benefits for your child, as it will teach them to focus on what is happening at that moment and break down the sensory overload they might experience. It can reduce the number of meltdowns your child will have and help you stay calm when your child does have one.

Practicing mindfulness with your child can also be a helpful bonding tool and build the trust that you need in your relationship with your child. What's more, other family members can also easily join in during these activities. Together, you can focus on what you're feeling, how you're feeling, accepting your emotions and thoughts, and regaining the calm you so desperately want in your home.

In this book, we've discussed many mindful techniques you can help your child with. Now, let's look at five of my favorite mindful activities that the whole family can do together.

RELAXING BODY SCANS

The first activity, "Body Scans," is a form of guided meditation that can help reduce anxiety. It forces you to connect your mind and body, and resist the urge to react to sensations you might feel. If your child is very hyperactive, this will also teach them that they're capable of sitting still and being quiet. Here's how you can use this technique:

- Before you start this scan, ask your child how they're feeling overall.
- Find a quiet, comfortable place where you can either sit or lie down. Try to keep your spine as straight as possible.
- Make sure your head is supported, either by a headrest or against a wall. I find it best to bend your knees so that your feet are planted firmly on the floor or on the bed.

- Once you're comfortable, notice all the places where your body is touching the floor, a chair, or a bed.

- Close your eyes or lower your gaze if this feels more comfortable. If your child is still new at this, you can keep an eye on them to make sure they follow the steps. Once they get used to this technique, you'll be able to close your eyes with them.

- Focus on one body part at a time. Pay attention to what you're feeling while breathing deeply.

- Start with your feet and move to your ankles, lower legs, knees, thighs, hips, pelvis, stomach, chest, shoulders, neck, face, head, upper arms, elbows, lower arms, wrists, and finish off with the hands. Breathe deeply while you feel the sensation in each body part. If you're doing this with your child, say the name of the body part you'll focus on next. Keep the tone of your voice as steady and low as possible to help set them into a relaxing rhythm.

- Now, focus on sections of your body, such as the entire top half, the entire bottom half, the entire left half, and the entire right half.

- Finish this exercise by focusing on your entire body for a few breaths.

- If you have any thoughts other than the sensations in your body while doing this, accept them and move on. Now is not the time to harp on the thoughts you might have.
- Once the body scan is complete, discuss with your child what they felt. Ask them how they're feeling after the scan, and compare this to their feelings before the scan. This can be helpful for them to realize how focusing on single sensations can benefit their overall well-being.

Depending on the severity of your child's condition, they might be able to do this scan by themselves after practicing it with you. Eventually, they might even be able to do it in the middle of a store when they become aware that they're feeling overwhelmed.

DO SOME MINDFUL WALKING

This is another great technique to help you become more aware of how your body moves and how you feel as you move. It is known to reduce anxiety and is another exercise that can be performed anywhere: indoors at home, outside in the garden, or even in a shop.

The purpose of this exercise is to bring attention to the sensations of your feet as you walk. It helps you calm down, become more aware of your body, and improve coordination between your muscles, joints, and tendons. Here's how you can do this:

- Take your child for a slow walk, preferably in bare feet. If you have lots of space, you can walk freely, but if your space is limited, walk in the shape of an eight.
- Start out slowly and pay attention to how your body weight moves from your heel to your toes as you take a step. Settle into a slow rhythm as you walk.
- Next, focus on the sensations and the different textures as you walk from the floor to carpet or from grass to concrete.
- If you want, bring some fun in by pretending to walk through mud or on hot coals. If your child is interested in space, you can even pretend to walk on the moon.
- Focus on the sensations on your feet, your legs, your hips, and your upper body. Mix up the pace by going from a slow walk, to a brisk walk, and back to slow again.
- Once you're feeling relaxed, you can finish your walk by returning to your starting point.

CREATE A GLITTER JAR

Creating a glitter jar is another effective way to teach children mindfulness by being creative. It can help to create a connection between your child's thoughts and feelings, help to bring calmness into their lives, and encourage them to behave in a socially more acceptable manner. Here's how you do this:

- Take a container with a leak-proof lid. This can be a glass jar or a plastic bottle, as long as it's clear.
- Let your child choose three different colors of glitter. These glitters will represent their feelings, thoughts, and behaviors.
- Pour water into your container. You might want to add a few drops of glycerin to help the glitter float. Next, add the glitter to the water.
- Ask your child to name situations that make them feel nervous or frustrated.
- Once they have a specific scenario in mind, let them swirl the glitter in the bottle. Explain to them that just like the glitter is all jumbled up, so can their thoughts, feelings, and behaviors get.
- Now, let them put the glitter jar down and watch how the glitter slowly drops to the

bottom. Just like the glitter is slowly dropping and calmness is returning to the jar, so can their thoughts, feelings, and behaviors become calm if they focus on staying calm.

Let them use this glitter jar they've made whenever they're feeling overwhelmed. You can even let them make a few glitter jars so that you can keep jars in their calm down caddies as well.

EYE PALMING

If your child is a visual learner, the chances are good that their eyes will get tired during the day. This can easily lead to meltdowns, fatigue, and headaches. You can help your child soothe their optic nerves by doing eye palming, which is basically like meditation for your eyes. While this helps their eyes to relax, it can have a calming effect over their entire body. Here's how you can do this:

- Sit somewhere comfortable, ideally at a table where you can rest your elbows for support.
- Rub your hands together until you feel your palms warming up.
- Once your palms are warm, close your eyes and cup your eyes with your eyes. Be careful not to

press on your eye sockets or cheekbones, as this
can not only be distracting but also be harmful.

- Visualize seeing blackness while breathing
  slowly and deeply.
- If you see any colors or lights, your optic nerve
  is likely irritated. If it's possible, stay in this
  position until the lights or colors disappear.

Since this is such a quick and easy exercise to do, your
child can do it a few times every day. I would recommend you do this with your child before you teach
them a new skill, especially if you're going to use visual
prompts. This will help them to increase their focus
and avoid trying to concentrate with tired and sore
eyes.

5-4-3-2-1 MINDFULNESS

This is another quick and easy technique your child
will be able to do anywhere (even in the middle of the
store) to help them calm down, manage their anxiety,
and reduce their anger. By using this technique and
focusing only on certain things, they will be able to
reduce the overwhelm they might experience in certain
situations. This can also be a fun activity that the whole
family can do together.

Here's how you do it:

- Let your child look around and find
- five things that they can see.
- four things that they can touch.
- three things that they can hear.
- two things that they can smell.
- one thing that they can taste.

Let them name everything out loud or point to the things they're listing. Apart from calming them down and reducing their anxiety and overwhelm, this will also help to give you a good idea of the level of sensory under- or oversensitivity they might be experiencing on that day.

CONSIDERING SOCIAL SKILLS GROUPS

If you find that your child's abilities are improving by practicing the techniques mentioned in this book, you can consider boosting your child's social skills by letting them join social skills groups. These groups are often presented in schools specializing in ASD and allow children to receive lessons in a social environment. During these sessions, your child will be taught social skills through different structures, play, social scenarios, and role-playing. It can help improve your child's self-awareness and help them become more aware of the feelings of others.

Let's look at some of the other benefits these groups can have for your child:

- They will learn more social skills, including having conversations, understanding body language, and showing empathy.
- They will learn more problem-solving skills by working in groups to do activities.
- Their self-confidence will develop as they feel like they belong.
- They will learn in a safe space surrounded by their peers.
- They will learn that they can have fun while playing with other children.

These social groups also hold a benefit for you as a parent: You will have some much-needed free time to reflect and practice self-care.

CONCLUSION

You now have all the skills you need to help your child manage the symptoms of their ASD more successfully, become more mindful, manage their emotions better, and cope with the social difficulties they may experience. You have a better understanding of their ASD and the potential impact their symptoms can have on their lives, and as a result, you understand your child a lot better.

You realize what a positive effect being more mindful in your parenting style can have on your child and how important it is to adjust your style to protect and enhance your child's mental wellness. You understand the massive impact that DBT techniques—and its four pillars: mindfulness, interpersonal effectiveness, distress tolerance, and emotional regulation—can have not only on your child's ability to cope with their condition but also to reduce the daily stress you're likely experiencing.

You can be the parent you've always wanted to be. You can have a happy and successful child despite having ASD. You can help your child through the difficult symptoms they may experience. You now have all the tools and techniques you will need to achieve this. Go out there, use them, and create the life and relationship with your child that you've always desired.

If you enjoyed the book and found the exercises and tips provided to be life changing for you and your child, please help me to assist others by leaving a review on Amazon.

REFERENCES

ADHD and Autism Spectrum Disorder. (n.d.). Children and Adults with Attention Deficit Hyperactivity Disorder. https://chadd.org/about-adhd/adhd-and-autism- spectrum-disorder

Anand, N. (2021, February 20). *Common challenges of parenting an autistic child.* Codleo. https://caliberautism.com/blog/Common-Challenges-of-Parenting-an-Autistic-Child

Autism and mental health. (n.d.). Mental Health. https://www.mentalhealth.org.uk /explore-mental-health/a-z-topics/autism-and-mental-health

Autism myths and stereotypes. (n.d.). In Understanding Autism. https://www.autismeducationtrust.org.uk/sites/default/files/2021-12/autismmyths.pdf

Autism spectrum disorder - Symptoms and causes. (2018, January 6). Mayo Clinic. https://www.mayoclinic.org/diseases-conditions/autism-spectrum-disorder/symptoms-causes/syc-20352928

Autism: signs in older children and teenagers. (n.d.). Raising Children Network. https://raisingchildren.net.au/autism/learning-about-autism/assessment-diagnosis/signs-of-asd-in-teens

Brazier, Y. (2016, November 2). *Autism: Parents face challenges, too.* Medical News Today. https://www.medicalnewstoday.com/articles/313789

Butter, E. (2017, April 21). *Autism spectrum disorders: The difference between boys and girls.* Nationwide Children's. https://www.nationwidechildrens.org/family-resources-education/700childrens/2017/04/autism-spectrum-disorders-the-difference-between-boys-and-girls

Challenging behaviour: Children and teenagers with autism spectrum disorder. (2017, June 5). Raising Children Network. https://raisingchildren.net.au/autism/behaviour/understanding-behaviour/challenging-behaviour-asd

Common challenges. (2022). Autism Tasmania. https://www.autismtas.org.au/about-autism/common-challenges/

Communication: children with autism spectrum disorder. (2017, October). Raising Children Network. https://raisingchildren.net.au/autism/communicating -relationships/communicating/communication-asd

Copeland, J. N. (2021, August). *What is autism spectrum disorder?* American Psychiatric Association. https://www.psychiatry.org/patients-families/autism/ what-is-autism-spectrum-disorder

Costello, R. (2021, January 30). *8 simple and accessible mindfulness activities for autism.* Yo Re Mi. https://www.yoremikids.com/news/mindfulness-for-autism

Courchesne, E. (2004). *Brain development in autism: Early overgrowth followed by premature arrest of growth.* Mental Retardation and Developmental Disabilities Research Reviews, 10(2), 106–111. https://doi.org/10.1002/mrdd.20020

Debunking 8 common stereotypes of individuals with autism. (2021, September 16). Autism Learning Partners. https://www.autismlearningpartners.com/ debunking-8-common-stereotypes-of-individuals-with-autism

Depression. (n.d.). National Autistic Society. https://www.autism.org.uk/advice-and- guidance/topics/mental-health/depression

Dialectical behavior therapy. (n.d.). Psychology Today. https://www.psychologytoday.com/us/therapy-types/ dialectical-behavior-therapy?amp

Dialectical behavior therapy (DBT). (2022, April 19). Cleveland Clinic. https://my.clevelandclinic.org/ health/treatments/22838-dialectical-behavior-therapy-dbt

Dialectical behavioral therapy and autism: An empowering set of skills. (2019, August 23). NeuroClastic. https:// neuroclastic.com/dialectical-behavioral-therapy- therapy-autism-an-empowering-set-of-skills/?amp

Eight self-care ideas for parents of autistic children during the holidays. (n.d.). Applied Behavior Analysis Programs Guide. Retrieved December 15, 2022, from https:// www.appliedbehavioranalysisprograms.com/lists/5-self-care-ideas-for-parents-of-autistic-children-during-the-holidays/

Five benefits of social skills groups. (2019, September 26). Autism Alliance. http://www.autismalliance.com.au/5-benefits-of-social-skills-groups/

Five DBT skills to help your kids manage stress. (n.d.). Idaho Youth Ranch. https://www.youthranch.org/blog/5-dbt-skills-to-help-your-kids-manage-stress? hs_amp=true

Grohol, J. M., & Telloian, C. (2022, August 24). *Autism symptoms: Patterns of communication and behavior.* Psych Central. https://psychcentral.com/autism/autism-spectrum-disorder-symptoms

Hoffman, M. (2020, December 6). *What are the types of autism spectrum disorder?* WebMD. https://www.webmd.com/brain/autism/autism-spectrum-disorders

How autism spectrum disorder affects learning and development. (2020, July 5). Raising Children Network. https://raisingchildren.net.au/autism/learning-about-autism/about-autism/how-asd-affects-development

How to help children with autism handle their emotions. (2021, July 29). LuxAI. https://luxai.com/blog/emotional-regulation-calm-down-activities-for-autistic-children/#useful-tips-for-parents-to-help-children-with-emotional-regulation

How to improve emotional self-regulation among children with autism and attention disorders. (2018, December 3). Pepperdine Online Programs. https://onlinegrad.pepperdine.edu/blog/emotional-self-regulation-children-autism/

How to love your child with autism when they don't (seem to) love you back. (n.d.). Exceptional Lives. https://www.exceptionallives.org/blog/how-to-love-your-child-autism?format=amp

Huntjens, A., van den Bosch, L. M. C. W., Sizoo, B., Kerkhof, A., Huibers, M. J. H., & van der Gaag, M. (2020). *The effect of dialectical behaviour therapy in autism spectrum patients with suicidality and/ or self-destructive behaviour (DIASS): study protocol for a multicentre randomised controlled trial.* BMC Psychiatry, 20(1). https://doi.org/10.1186/s12888-020-02531-1

Hurley, K. (2022, February 2). *How to improve communication with your ASD child.* Psycom.net. https://www.psycom.net/autism-communication

Hus, Y., & Segal, O. (2021). Challenges surrounding the diagnosis of autism in children. *Neuropsychiatric Disease and Treatment, 17,* 3509–3529. https://doi.org/10.2147/NDT.S282569

Importance of being your child's cheerleader. (2019, November 7). Blossom Children's Center. https://blossomchildrenscenter.com/2019/11/07/the- importance-of-being-your-childs-cheerleader/

Long, J. (2011, May 10). *Autism: A lesson in compassion.* Patch. https://patch.com/california/alisoviejo/autism-a-lesson-in-compassion-4

McIlwee, C. (n.d.). *First steps after receiving an autism diagnosis.* JCFS Chicago. https://www.jcfs.org/blog/first-steps-after-receiving-autism-diagnosis

Milam, S. (2021, November 19). *When my son with autism melts down, here's what I do.* Healthline. https://www.healthline.com/health/autism/what-to-do-autism-meltdown#What-to-do-during-a-very-loud

Obinna, C. (2016, June 28). *How autism affects your child — Experts.* Vanguard News. https://www.vanguardngr.com/2016/06/autism-affects-child-experts/

Omahen, E. (2020, March 4). *Easy ways to help your child with self-regulation.* Autism Parenting Magazine. https://www.autismparentingmagazine.com/easy-ways -with-self-regulation/

Panol, A. (2020, July 26). *How to document your child's progress.* The Autism Community in Action (TACA). https://tacanow.org/family-resources/how-to- docu-ment-your-childs-progress/

Pathak, N. (2021, September 21). *What is autism?* WebMD. https://www.webmd.com/brain/autism/understanding-autism-basics

Positive relationships in families with autistic children. (n.d.). Raising Children Network. https://raisingchildren.net.au/autism/communicating-relationships/family-relationships/family-relationships-asd

Problem solving activities for kids with autism. (2022). Study.com. https://study.com/academy/lesson/problem-solving-activities-for-kids-with-autism.html

Rowden, A. (2021, November 23). *What are the types of autism?* Medical News Today. https://www.medicalnewstoday.com/articles/types-of-autism#diagnosis-and-levels

Rudy, L. J. (2022a, January 21). *Autistic children and developmental milestones*. Verywell Health. https://www.verywellhealth.com/developmental-milestones-in-children-with-autism-4128725

Rudy, L. J. (2022b, October 16). *Why do autistic children stim?* Verywell Health. https://www.verywellhealth.com/what-is-stimming-in-autism-260034

Selbst, M. (2014, July 1). *Social Problem Solving: Best Practices for Youth with ASD*. Autism Spectrum News. https://autismspectrumnews.org/social-problem-solving-best-practices-for-youth-with-asd/

Sensory differences - a guide for all audiences. (2020, September 2). National Autistic Society. https://www.autism.org.uk/advice-and-guidance/topics/sensory-differences/sensory-differences/all-audiences

Signs and symptoms of autism spectrum disorders. (2022, March 28). Centers for Disease Control and Prevention. https://www.cdc.gov/ncbddd/autism/ signs.html

Signs of autism in different age groups and genders. (2020, June 3). Otsimo. https://otsimo.com/en/10-early-signs-of-autism-in-different-age-groups/

Smith, K. (2020, February 5). *Coping with stress while caring for a child with autism.* Psycom. https://www. psycom.net/coping-with-stress-while-caring-for-a-child- with-autism

Smith, M., Segal, J., & Hutman, T. (2019, March 20). *Helping your child with autism thrive.* HelpGuide. https:// www.helpguide.org/articles/autism-learning- disabilities/helping-your-child-with-autism-thrive.htm

Social skills for children with autism spectrum disorder. (2017, August 2). Raising Children Network. https:// raisingchildren.net.au/autism/communicating- relationships/connecting/social-skills-for-children-with-asd

Talton, L. (2021, September 3). *Five social skills activities for children with autism.* Autism Parenting Magazine. https://www.autismparentingmagazine.com/ five-social-skills-activities/

Tamara. (2022, July 24). *How to manage your stress as a parent of an autistic and ADHD child.* Autism & ADHD Connection. https://autismadhdconnection.com/ how-to-manage-your-stress-as-a-parent-of-an-autistic-and-adhd-child/

Ten ways to build independence. (2018, September 2). Autism Speaks. https://www.autismspeaks.org/tool-kit-excerpt/ten-ways-build-independence

Ten mindfulness activities you can try today. (2018, January 14). Pathway 2 Success. https://www.thepathway2suc cess.com/10-mindfulness-activities-you-can-try-today/

Thinking and learning strengths in children with autism spectrum disorder. (2021, July 26). Raising Children Network. https://raisingchildren.net.au/autism/ learn-ing-about-autism/about-autism/learning-strengths-asd

Twelve ways you can make your autistic child feel loved and accepted. (2017, September 21). The Autism Site. https://blog.theautismsite.greatergood.com/cs-child-loved-accepted/

Twenty famous people with autism spectrum disorder (ASD). (2021, July 14). Behavioral Innovations. https://behav ioral-innovations.com/blog/20-famous-people-with-autism-spectrum-disorder-asd/

What is autism spectrum disorder? (2020, March 25). Centers for Disease Control and Prevention. https://www.cdc.gov/ncbddd/autism/facts.html

When do children usually show symptoms of autism? (2017, January 31). National Institute for Child Health and Human Development. https://www.nichd.nih.gov/health/topics/autism/conditioninfo/symptoms-appear

White, T. (2022, May 9). *Autism and social skills: Seeing the world differently.* Psych Central. https://psychcentral.com/autism/autism-social-skills

Made in United States
Troutdale, OR
09/02/2023

12490082R00119